GCSE English

Of Mice and Men

by John Steinbeck

Studying English texts can give you a real headache,
but happily this CGP book makes your life just a little bit easier.

This book has everything you need to write a brilliant essay about *Of Mice and Men*.
It doesn't just tell you what happens — it's got analysis of the main characters,
themes, historical background and language features too.

Plus, there are plenty of practice questions and a worked exam answer
with tips on how to improve your grade on the big day.

And of course, we've done our best to make the whole
experience at least vaguely entertaining for you.

The Text Guide

Foundation Level

CONTENTS

CONTENTS

Published by CGP

Editors:
David Broadbent
Heather Gregson
Rachael Powers
Holly Poynton
Caley Simpson
Rebecca Tate

Contributors:
Peter Needham

With thanks to Glenn Rogers and Nicola Woodfin for the proofreading
and Laura Jakubowski and Laura Stoney for the copyright research.

Acknowledgements:

Cover Illustration by Adrian McOran-Campbell © 2011

With thanks to Rex Features for permission to use the images on pages 1, 2, 4, 7, 8, 10, 18, 26 & 39

Photographs on pages 3, 4, 15, 16, 17, 19, 20, 28, 30, 36, 37, 44 & 46 © James Cotton
Photographs are from the Uwharrie Players Theatre production of Of Mice & Men directed by Craig Kolkebeck

With thanks to Ben Franske, Franske Consulting LLC, for permission to use the photographs
on pages 3, 5, 11, 14, 21, 27, 29, 32, 33, 41, 45 & 47. Photographs are from the
Winter 2007 Edina High School Theatre Production of Of Mice and Men

With thanks to Mikki Schaffner of Schaffner Studios for permission to use the photographs of Northern
Kentucky University's production of Of Mice and Men on pages 3: Tim Rhoades as Boss (edited), 5: (Left to
Right) Matt Bohnert as George Milton & Nick Vannoy as Lennie (edited), 13: (Left to Right) Nick Vannoy as
Lennie & Matt Bohnert as George Milton, 25: (Left to Right) Matt Bohnert as George Milton & Dean Muir as
Curly, 31: (Left to Right) Jack Burrows as Whit, Aaron Brewer as Slim & Sean Harkless as Candy (edited), 38:
(Left to Right) Matt Bohnert as George Milton & Emma Robertson as Curly's Wife, 40: Emma Robertson as
Curly's Wife (edited) & 46: (Left to Right) Sean Harkless as Candy & Ricky Glore as Carlson (edited)

With thanks to Photofest for permission to use the images on pages 4, 5, 12, 36 & 39

With thanks to iStockphoto.com for permission to use the image on page 5

With thanks to Mary Evans Picture Library for permission to use the image on page 6

With thanks to Alamy for permission to use the image on page 24

Extract on page 52 from Of Mice and Men by John Steinbeck (Penguin, 2000).
Copyright © John Steinbeck, 1937, 1965. Reproduced by permission of Penguin Books Ltd.

ISBN: 978 1 84762 721 6
Website: www.cgpbooks.co.uk
Printed by Elanders Ltd, Newcastle upon Tyne.
Clipart from CorelDRAW®

Based on the classic CGP style created by Richard Parsons.

Introduction to 'Of Mice and Men' and John Steinbeck

'Of Mice and Men' is about the **lives** of **farm workers**

- *Of Mice and Men* is a novel about two <u>farm workers</u> and their dream of having their <u>own farm</u>.

- The title of the novel comes from <u>Robert Burns's</u> poem, '<u>To a Mouse</u>'. In the poem Burns wrote that, "The best-laid schemes o' mice an' men / Gang aft agley" — this means that even really well-prepared plans <u>often go wrong</u>.

- The <u>characters</u> and <u>events</u> in the novel <u>aren't real</u> — but they show what life was like during the <u>Great Depression</u>.

The Great Depression

1) The <u>Great Depression</u> in America was a time when <u>businesses struggled</u> and many people didn't have a <u>job</u>.

2) It started when the stock market in the USA <u>crashed</u> in 1929. This meant that <u>businesses failed</u> and millions of people were <u>unemployed</u>.

3) Many people had to <u>travel</u> across the country looking for <u>jobs</u>, like temporary farm work.

4) They were paid very <u>low wages</u> and stayed in <u>poor accommodation</u>.

Two migrant workers looking for jobs during the Great Depression.

© Everett Collection / Rex Features

John Steinbeck knew what **life** on **ranches** was like

Of Mice and Men is partly based on John Steinbeck's <u>own experiences</u> working on ranches while he was at university.

1902	Born in <u>Salinas</u>, California.
1919	Went to <u>Stanford University</u>. He spent his summers working as a <u>ranch hand</u>.
1929	The <u>stock market</u> in the USA <u>crashed</u>. This was the start of the <u>Great Depression</u>.
1937	Published '<u>Of Mice and Men</u>'. It was an <u>instant success</u>.
1962	Awarded the <u>Nobel Prize in Literature</u>.
1968	Died, aged 66.

© Sipa Press / Rex Features

Background Information

'Of Mice and Men' is set on a **ranch** in **California**

Weed and Soledad are both <u>real places</u> in California in the USA, though the <u>ranch</u> where George and Lennie work is <u>made up</u>. This map shows where <u>California</u> is, and how the ranch <u>might have looked</u>.

To Weed

To Soledad

The Barn

The Harness Room

Curley's House

The Bunk House

USA

California

The Clearing

The Pool

Farmers struggled in the **Great Depression**

- Before the Great Depression, lots of farmers had <u>borrowed money</u> from banks to help them buy new machines.

- After the stock market crashed, lots of <u>banks</u> were in trouble and needed their money <u>back</u>. Farmers <u>couldn't afford</u> to pay them back. Many farmers had to <u>sell</u> their farms.

- There was a <u>long drought</u> in the 1930s. For ten years there wasn't enough <u>rain</u> to grow healthy crops, the land became <u>dry</u> and <u>winds</u> blew away the <u>good soil</u>. This time became known as the '<u>Dust Bowl</u>' era.

A farmer and his sons walking through the dusty landscape in 1936.

Who's Who on the Ranch

George...

...is a farm worker. He's small and quite clever. He travels around with his friend, Lennie.

© Mikki Schaffner

Lennie...

...is a big, strong man who isn't that clever. He travels with George. He likes stroking soft things.

© Ben Franske

Candy...

...is an old, one-handed ranch worker who sweeps the bunk house. He has an old, smelly dog.

© James Cotton

Crooks...

...is a crippled man who's picked on because he's black. He's very bitter about his life.

© James Cotton

Slim...

...is the most respected man on the ranch. Everyone looks up to him.

© James Cotton

Curley...

...is a small man who likes fighting and hates big guys. He's the boss's son and no one likes him.

© Ben Franske

Curley's wife...

...is young, pretty and a bit of a flirt. She hates her life on the ranch and she's very lonely.

© Mikki Schaffner

Carlson...

...is an uncaring, insensitive ranch worker. He's always stirring up trouble on the ranch.

© Mikki Schaffner

'Of Mice and Men' — Plot Summary

'Of Mice and Men'... what happens when?

Here's a little recap of the main events of *Of Mice and Men*. It's a good idea to learn what happens when, so that you know exactly how all the important events fit together.

Chapter One — *the calm before the storm*

Lennie and George by the pool.

- George and Lennie are two friends who travel together looking for farm work during the Great Depression.

- They're spending the night by a pool. The next day they start work at a new ranch.

- George is annoyed with Lennie because they had to leave their last job in a hurry.

- Lennie persuades George to tell him about their dream farm. It sounds like a really safe and happy place.

Chapter Two — *introductions*

- George and Lennie arrive at the ranch late — the boss is angry.

- George and Lennie meet all the main people on the ranch, including Candy, Curley, Curley's wife and Slim.

- Curley tries to pick a fight with Lennie.

- Curley's wife flirts with the ranchers and catches Lennie's attention.

The boss with George and Lennie.

Chapter Three — *dreams and a dead dog*

Curley gets ready to attack Lennie.

- Slim promises Lennie one of his dog's new puppies.

- Carlson wants to shoot Candy's dog because it's old and smelly. Candy's forced to agree even though he doesn't want to.

- Carlson takes the dog away and shoots it.

- Candy hears George and Lennie talking about their dream farm. He asks to join them, and offers them his money.

- Curley starts a fight with Lennie and Lennie crushes his hand.

Chapter Four — the dream is spoiled

- Lennie goes into <u>Crooks's room</u>. <u>Candy</u> joins them.

- They talk about the <u>dream farm</u>. Crooks says he'd like to <u>work</u> on the <u>dream farm</u> too.

- <u>Curley's wife</u> comes in and <u>taunts</u> them. When Candy stands up to her she makes their dream <u>sound silly</u> and says it'll <u>never happen</u>.

- Crooks says he's <u>not interested</u> in the farm any more.

Candy gets angry with Curley's wife.

Chapter Five — a dead girl and a dead dream

Lennie talks to Curley's wife in the barn.

- Lennie is in the <u>barn</u> — he's <u>killed</u> his <u>puppy</u> by mistake.

- <u>Curley's wife</u> finds him and they talk about their <u>dreams</u>.

- Curley's wife lets Lennie <u>stroke her hair</u>, but she gets <u>angry</u> when he strokes it <u>too hard</u>.

- Lennie <u>panics</u> and breaks her neck by accident.

- Lennie <u>runs away</u>. Curley and the other men decide to <u>hunt</u> Lennie down and <u>kill</u> him.

Chapter Six — George kills his best friend

- Lennie goes back to the <u>pool</u> where he and George stayed the night before they went to the ranch.

- George <u>finds</u> Lennie by the pool. He <u>calms</u> Lennie down by telling him about the <u>dream farm</u> again.

- George knows that <u>Curley</u> wants to <u>kill Lennie</u> in a really <u>painful</u> way. He wants revenge for Lennie <u>crushing</u> his <u>hand</u> and <u>killing</u> his <u>wife</u>.

- George shoots Lennie <u>himself</u> before the other men arrive.

George finds Lennie by the pool.

'Of Mice and Men' — a story about mice... and men

Phew — a whole book is a lot to cram into a couple of pages... The next section is all about the time the novel is set in, so grab a quick cup of tea and then it's time to read on. If you're still not sure about the novel's plot or want something to do while the kettle's boiling, have a look at the cartoon at the back of the book.

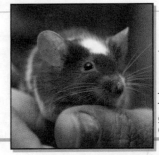

America in the 1930s

In the 1930s, America was in a mess — the economy was in trouble and lots of people were unemployed... Knowing what life was like in the 1930s will help you understand why this novel was so popular.

In the 1920s the American **economy** was doing well...

New York in the 1920s.

The 1920s was a time of <u>riches</u> and <u>comfort</u> for America — the <u>economy</u> was doing really well.

- <u>Businesses</u> were really <u>successful</u>.

- There was <u>low unemployment</u> and most people lived comfortable lives.

- More people could <u>afford</u> things like radios, fridges and washing machines.

...but in **1929** it all went **wrong**

1) The American <u>stock market</u> crashed in 1929.

2) This means that the <u>value</u> of businesses <u>dropped suddenly</u>. People who'd bought <u>shares</u> in these businesses <u>lost</u> lots of <u>money</u>.

3) This led to a huge <u>economic depression</u> in the 1930s.

4) A <u>depression</u> is when the <u>economy</u> of a country gets <u>smaller</u> because businesses make <u>less money</u>. In the <u>1930s</u>:

> The <u>stock market</u> lets people buy a part of a <u>business</u> (<u>shares</u>). If the business <u>does well</u>, these people make <u>money</u> — but if the business does <u>badly</u>, they can <u>lose everything</u> they put in.

The depression in the 1930s was so bad it's normally called the Great Depression.

- Lots of businesses had to <u>close down</u> — so lots of people <u>lost</u> their <u>jobs</u>.
- People couldn't <u>pay back</u> money they <u>owed</u> to the banks.
- Many people <u>lost</u> their <u>homes</u> and lived in <u>poverty</u>.

'Of Mice and Men' was **written** during the **Great Depression**

1) John Steinbeck wrote *Of Mice and Men* in <u>1937</u> — right in the <u>middle</u> of the <u>Great Depression</u>.

2) It was really <u>popular straight away</u> because he wrote about <u>normal people</u>.

3) The characters in the novel are in the <u>same situation</u> as many people <u>during the depression</u>.

> - They don't have a <u>home</u> or a <u>permanent job</u>.
> - They don't have much <u>money</u> and they don't <u>own</u> many things.
> - They have to <u>travel around</u> to find work because there aren't many <u>jobs</u>.

4) Lots of people could <u>imagine</u> what <u>life</u> was like for these men.

America in the 1930s

Before the depression, many people thought America was a place where you could be successful and rich. However, the depression changed people's ideas of America — life was really tough for most people.

Travelling farm workers had **hard** lives

1) <u>Farmers</u> were <u>badly hit</u> by the Great Depression. Lots of them had <u>borrowed</u> money from <u>banks</u> to buy their farms.

2) When the <u>stock market</u> crashed in 1929, lots of banks asked for this <u>money back</u> but most farmers couldn't <u>afford</u> it.

3) Many farms <u>closed down</u> and farm workers lost their <u>jobs</u>.

4) Lots of these workers <u>travelled</u> around to try and find work.

> <u>George</u> and <u>Lennie</u> are examples of <u>travelling</u> farm workers. They travel around <u>California</u> looking for work on farms.

A travelling farm worker in 1938.

5) These workers took <u>temporary</u> jobs wherever they could find them. They <u>moved on</u> when the work was finished. They got a <u>bed</u> on the farm and some <u>food</u> but they weren't <u>paid</u> very much.

6) They often travelled <u>alone</u>, like many of the ranch workers in *Of Mice and Men*.

American society was **racist** in the **1930s**

<u>Crooks</u> is treated pretty <u>badly</u> in the book (see p.29 and 37). His experience was probably <u>similar</u> to lots of black men in America in the <u>1930s</u> — it was a very <u>racist</u> place.

1) <u>Racist language</u> is seen as very <u>insulting</u> now. It was quite <u>common</u> then.

> There's a lot of <u>racist language</u> in the book — Crooks is often called "Nigger".

2) There was <u>segregation</u> in many US states. This meant that <u>black</u> people weren't allowed to use the same schools, parks or hospitals as <u>white</u> people.

> Crooks is forced to <u>live separately</u> from the other ranch workers.

Women were less important than **men** in 1930s America

1) In 1930s America, women weren't <u>treated</u> the <u>same</u> as men.

2) Women were <u>expected</u> to <u>obey</u> their husbands.

> In *Of Mice and Men* <u>Curley</u> doesn't treat his wife very well. He doesn't care how <u>unhappy</u> she is.

3) Their <u>job</u> was to be a <u>good wife</u> — to look after the house and the <u>children</u>. Carlson tells <u>Curley</u> that he should get his <u>wife</u> to stay at home "<u>where she belongs</u>".

The Great Depression — well, the name really suited it...

One ray of sunshine — this book made John Steinbeck an instant success. Although his characters are depressed and miserable, you can take comfort in the fact that in real life, John Steinbeck's dream of being a writer came true. Awww.

The American Dream

Dreams are an important theme in *Of Mice and Men* (see p.39). The American Dream is also an important part of American society. It gave people something to work towards even when their lives were really hard.

The **American Dream** is about **freedom**

1) In the 1800s <u>most</u> of western America hadn't been <u>explored</u>. <u>Hardly anyone</u> lived there.

2) Many people from <u>other countries</u> saw America as a place where they could <u>start again</u> and have a new life.

3) During the 1800s they <u>travelled</u> to western America and settled on the <u>empty land</u>.

> Many people thought that in America you could be your <u>own boss</u> and make your <u>own fortune</u>. This was their <u>American Dream</u>.

The American Dream **fell apart** during the **Great Depression**

Man looking for work during the Great Depression.

© CPL Archv / Everett / Rex Features

1) By 1900 there was <u>no more</u> new <u>land</u> in western America to build on.

2) People needed something else to <u>hope</u> for. While the <u>economy</u> was doing <u>well</u> in the 1920s there was a <u>new</u> American Dream.

3) Putting <u>money</u> into the <u>stock market</u> seemed to be a way of getting <u>rich quickly</u>.

4) The <u>rise of Hollywood</u> also made people want <u>glamorous</u> and <u>exciting</u> lives.

> In the <u>1920s</u>, more people were going to the <u>cinema</u>. Hollywood stars became more <u>famous</u> and made more <u>money</u>.

5) The Great Depression <u>ended</u> this time of <u>confidence</u>. American people didn't have much to be <u>happy</u> about.

6) A bad <u>drought</u> in 1930, too much <u>farming</u> and <u>strong winds</u> ruined the land — this made it almost <u>impossible</u> to grow crops. Many farm workers travelled west to California to find work.

George and **Lennie** have their own **American Dream**

Theme — Dreams

> Crooks says that <u>other</u> farm workers have the <u>same dream</u> as George and Lennie — "<u>Ever'body</u> wants a little piece of <u>lan'</u>." In the end <u>no one's</u> dream comes <u>true</u> though — "<u>nobody</u> gets no land".

1) Life for George and Lennie is <u>tough</u> because they have to <u>travel around</u> looking for work on different ranches.

2) They <u>hope</u> that one day they'll have a <u>farm of their own</u>.

3) They want to <u>work for themselves</u> and control their <u>own lives</u>. This is their <u>version</u> of the <u>American Dream</u>.

A dream and then depression — like waking up on Monday morning...

Everyone was pretty down in the dumps in the 1930s, especially after everything had been so great in the 1920s. The American Dream seemed further and further away as even very rich people lost everything in the Great Depression.

Practice Questions

So this is a bit of a shock — you're doing GCSE English and you've got to learn some history. You'll get marks for knowing about what was going on in the world at the time the book was written though. The questions on this page are here to help you remember the key facts. Write a few words or a sentence for the quick questions, and a paragraph for the in-depth ones.

Quick Questions

Q1   What happened to the American stock market in 1929?
       a) It crashed.   b) It did really well.   c) It stayed the same.

Q2   What was the economic depression in America in the 1930s called?

Q3   How is Crooks separated from the other workers?
       a) He's not allowed to talk to them.
       b) He has to sleep separately.
       c) He has to wear different clothes.

Q4   Write one word to describe the mood of the American people in the 1930s.

In-depth Questions

Q1   How did life in America change between the 1920s and 1930s?

Q2   Write a paragraph describing the life of a travelling farm worker.

Q3   What is George and Lennie's version of the American Dream?

Section One — Background and Context

Analysis of Chapter One — By the Pool

The novel starts with George and Lennie resting by a pool. It's the end of a hot day.

What happens in Chapter One

- Lennie and George are two friends who work and travel together.
- They spend the night by a pool before starting work on a ranch.
- George tells Lennie about the 'dream' farm they'll have in the future.

It's **beautiful** by the pool — but it's also **threatening**

Symbolism is when an object represents an idea. For more on symbolism see p.46.

1) The novel starts with a <u>peaceful</u> natural scene. It's <u>disturbed</u> by George and Lennie's arrival.

2) George thinks it's going to be "nice sleepin' here", but it's also a bit <u>threatening</u>. Earlier on there were <u>men shouting</u> and a fish was described as sinking "<u>mysteriously</u>" into the water.

Symbolism

Steinbeck shows that nature can be <u>dangerous</u> and <u>peaceful</u>.

3) George has to take a <u>dead</u> mouse off Lennie and throw it into the <u>darkening</u> brush. This shows that <u>not everything is as good as it seems</u>.

George and Lennie have been **friends** for **ages**

Language — Signs

There are lots of <u>signs</u> like this that make the <u>reader</u> think that the <u>story</u> won't <u>end well</u>.

1) When George and Lennie walk along, George <u>leads the way</u> and Lennie <u>follows</u> him. Lennie keeps <u>asking</u> George <u>questions</u>. These things make Lennie seem <u>childlike</u>.

2) The bus driver drops them off <u>four miles</u> away from the ranch. This is a sign that they <u>never</u> end up where they <u>want to be</u>.

3) You can tell George and Lennie know each other <u>really well</u>. George <u>knows</u> that Lennie is <u>lying</u> about having a mouse — "You ain't puttin' nothing over."

© Nigel R. Barklie / Rex Features

George walks along, with Lennie following him.

There's a lot of **animal imagery** in this chapter

Imagery is when words create a picture in your mind.

1) Lennie is compared to different <u>animals</u> in this chapter:

2) These are <u>strong</u> animals. This makes Lennie seem <u>powerful</u>. However, he also has the low <u>intelligence</u> of an animal.

3) When George <u>confronts</u> Lennie about the <u>mouse</u> Lennie looks "as though he contemplated running". Lennie's like an animal — he wants to <u>escape</u> when he's under <u>threat</u>.

Language — Imagery

- He walks like a "<u>bear</u>".
- He drinks "<u>like a horse</u>".
- He holds the mouse "<u>like a terrier</u>".

Analysis of Chapter One — By the Pool

George **tells** Lennie about the **dream**

1) Lennie gets <u>upset</u> when George is <u>angry</u>. George describes the 'dream' farm to Lennie to <u>calm</u> him down.

2) Lennie <u>loves</u> the dream, especially the part about the <u>rabbits</u>. George <u>doesn't</u> seem as enthusiastic. He <u>cuts the story short</u> — he says, "I ain't got time".

3) It's <u>not clear</u> at this point whether George <u>believes</u> in the dream. Sometimes he says he'd be <u>happy</u> without Lennie.

Theme — Dreams

George says that the <u>rabbits</u> on the <u>dream farm</u> would be "Red and blue and green rabbits". This makes the <u>dream</u> seem <u>unreal</u>.

This chapter is a **rollercoaster ride**

1) There are lots of <u>ups</u> and <u>downs</u> in this chapter. One moment George is <u>shouting</u> at Lennie, the next he's <u>comforting</u> him.

2) This tells the <u>reader</u> a lot about George's <u>personality</u>.

3) The <u>range of emotions</u> that George shows makes him seem more <u>realistic</u>. George can be:

Lennie and George talk by the pool.

© Ben Franske

Angry → George <u>shouts</u> at Lennie for killing the mouse.

Kind → George <u>comforts</u> Lennie and says he's sorry.

George wishes he was travelling <u>alone</u>.

George is <u>ashamed</u> of wanting Lennie to leave.

George tells Lennie to "<u>Shut up now</u>".

Steinbeck **hints** at what will happen **next**

Writers can hint at something that happens later in the story. This is called foreshadowing (see p.44).

1) George and Lennie are <u>on the run</u> from a "<u>bad thing</u>" that Lennie did in Weed. George has a <u>plan</u> to meet Lennie back at the <u>pool</u> in case Lennie gets in trouble again.

2) Here Steinbeck is <u>foreshadowing</u> what will happen at the <u>end of the novel</u>.

Theme — Destiny

George <u>seems to know</u> that he and Lennie will <u>need</u> to <u>come back</u> to the <u>pool in the future</u>.

<u>Lots</u> of other <u>people</u> have already made the <u>journey</u> that George and Lennie are <u>making</u>. This is shown by the <u>well worn</u> path to the pool. This makes it seem that there's <u>nothing special</u> about them or their dream.

Lennie's like a .... bear — why the long paws...

Lennie's movements and actions are described in animal-like terms. Steinbeck obviously wants us to know that Lennie's wild, strong and he's not easy to control. You gotta be careful with him because he might kill you...

Analysis of Chapter Two — Settling in on the Ranch

Lennie and George arrive at the ranch. All the characters are introduced, one by one.

What happens in Chapter Two

- George and Lennie meet the other ranch workers.
- The boss's son Curley seems to want to fight everyone.
- Curley's wife is really pretty and Lennie can't stop looking at her.

The men on the ranch *seem nice*...

Theme — Loneliness

George often plays 'solitaire' in the bunk house. This is a card game for one player — it's a sign of how lonely the men are.

1) Most of the ranch hands seem nice enough.

2) Candy is helpful, showing George and Lennie their beds and telling them about the other ranch hands.

3) Carlson is nice to George and Lennie and jokes that Lennie "ain't very small".

...but they can be *cruel* too

1) Candy is rude about Curley's wife. He calls her a "tart" and gossips about how she gives men "the eye" — she flirts with them.

2) Carlson is horrible about Candy's dog because it stinks "like hell". He wants Slim to get Candy to shoot the dog and take a puppy instead. He's pretty heartless.

3) The men talk about how they invited Crooks the "stable buck" into the bunk house at Christmas, and one of the ranchers picked a fight with him for no reason.

Symbolism

Carlson wants the dog to be shot because it's old and useless. Steinbeck is saying that no-one would care for ranch hands like Candy when they get old.

Theme — Prejudice

Crooks is picked on by the farm hands and the boss "gives him hell" when he's angry. He's treated this way because he's black.

The *boss* and Curley aren't *friendly*

1) The boss is suspicious because George won't let Lennie answer questions — "What you trying to put over?"

2) The boss's son, Curley, is even less welcoming.

He quizzes Lennie and George in an aggressive way. When he talks to Lennie, Curley's hands "closed into fists". It looks like he wants to punch Lennie.

3) George says that Curley's "gonna get hurt" if he messes with Lennie. This is a hint at what happens later on.

Curley talks to George.

MGM / Photofest © MGM

Analysis of Chapter Two — Settling in on the Ranch

Curley's wife **flirts** with **everyone**

The colour <u>red</u> is important. It's the colour of <u>danger</u> and <u>sex</u>. Curley's wife is linked to <u>both</u> of these things (see p.47).

1) Curley's wife has "<u>rouged lips</u>" (she's wearing red lipstick), <u>red</u> fingernails and "<u>red</u> mules" (shoes) with "<u>red</u> ostrich feathers".

2) The way that she <u>stands</u> — leaning against the doorpost and <u>tilting her body forwards</u> — shows that she knows she's <u>attractive</u>. She's trying to make the men <u>want her</u>.

3) Lennie says that Curley's wife is "<u>purty</u>". George warns him to <u>stay away</u> from her. He's <u>worried</u> about how Lennie might <u>act</u> around her.

Theme — Loneliness

Curley's wife says that she's <u>looking for Curley</u> at the bunk house. She probably just wants to <u>talk</u> to other <u>people</u> though.

Slim is the **nicest** man on the ranch

1) Slim seems <u>different</u> from the other ranch hands.

- He has "<u>majesty</u>".
- He's the "<u>prince</u> of the ranch".
- He has "<u>authority</u>".

Character — Slim

Steinbeck <u>describes</u> Slim like this to show that he's <u>respected</u> by the other men. He's a <u>good leader</u>.

2) He's <u>interested</u> in George and Lennie — he looks at them "kindly".

3) Everyone else has made George <u>jumpy</u>, but Slim <u>calms</u> him down.

4) Even Carlson knows Slim is <u>special</u> — he steps back to let Slim go <u>first</u> when it's dinner time.

George and Lennie are both **worried**

1) George <u>doesn't like</u> the ranch:

- He <u>shouts</u> at Lennie for talking to the boss. He doesn't want the boss to <u>find out</u> what happened in <u>Weed</u>.
- He's <u>scared</u> that Curley will pick a <u>fight</u> with Lennie.
- He's worried that <u>Curley's wife</u> will cause some <u>trouble</u>.

2) Even <u>Lennie</u> can tell that the ranch is a <u>dangerous</u> place — "I don' like this place... I wanna get outta here."

George tells Lennie they have to stay at the ranch.

© Mikki Schaffner

The name's Small, Lennie Small...

Lennie's called Small, but he's actually really big. Oh it's too funny... If these jokes get any funnier I'm going to have to stop reading *Of Mice and Men* and start my own joke shop. There aren't any more jokes? Oh, OK. Read on then...

Analysis of Chapter Three — The Dream and a Fight

It seems like the dream farm might actually happen — but then Curley ruins it by being an idiot.

What happens in Chapter Three

- Carlson persuades Candy to let him shoot Candy's dog.
- Candy offers George and Lennie some money for the dream farm.
- Curley starts a fight with Lennie. Lennie crushes Curley's hand.

George **opens up** to Slim

1) George <u>relaxes</u> and chats to Slim about his past while Lennie is playing with the puppies.

2) Lennie <u>wouldn't</u> be able to <u>survive</u> without someone looking after him — Slim says he's "jes' like a <u>kid</u>".

3) George thinks men who travel <u>alone</u> are lonely. It makes them get "<u>mean</u>" and want to "fight all the time".

4) George <u>explains</u> that Lennie gets into <u>trouble</u>:

In <u>Weed</u> Lennie grabbed a girl's <u>red</u> dress and wouldn't let go. The <u>red dress</u> reminds you of <u>Curley's wife</u> — she wears a lot of <u>red</u>. It's another <u>warning</u> that <u>danger</u> is coming.

Whit finds a **letter** in a **magazine**

1) Whit finds a <u>letter</u> in a magazine from an <u>old ranch hand</u>. He's really excited about such a <u>small thing</u> — this suggests that his life is <u>quite boring</u>.

2) He <u>invites</u> George to come with him and the other men to the <u>brothel</u> saying it's "a hell of a lot of fun".

Whit shows the reader what George <u>might be like</u> if he didn't have Lennie or their 'dream'.

George and Whit chat in the bunk house.

© Ben Franske

Candy's dog gets **killed**

1) Carlson wants to <u>shoot Candy's dog</u> — he says it "<u>stinks</u>".

2) It's only when <u>Slim</u> says that the dog should be killed that Candy <u>agrees</u>. This <u>shows</u> that everyone on the ranch <u>listens</u> to <u>Slim</u>.

3) It's really <u>awkward</u> in the bunk house while the men wait for Carlson to shoot Candy's dog. Candy's <u>sadness</u> about losing his dog makes everyone feel very <u>uncomfortable</u>.

Theme — Death

The way Carlson <u>shoots</u> Candy's dog <u>foreshadows</u> the way George <u>kills Lennie</u>.

Foreshadowing is a way of hinting at something that happens later in the story (see p.44).

Analysis of Chapter Three — The Dream and a Fight

There's a chance that the **dream** could come **true**

1) When Candy <u>hears</u> about George and Lennie's dream <u>farm</u> he offers them <u>money</u> to pay for the land. He <u>believes</u> in the <u>dream</u>.

2) George <u>works out</u> that they could buy the farm by the <u>end of the month</u>. He's <u>really excited</u> about it.

3) This is probably the most <u>hopeful</u> moment in the story. It makes what happens <u>next</u> in this chapter <u>even worse</u> because the dream seems so <u>close</u> to coming <u>true</u>.

Theme — Dreams

This is the <u>only time</u> George <u>believes</u> in the <u>dream</u> — "I bet we could swing her". For a moment he sees a <u>way out</u> of his depressing life.

Curley and Lennie's **fight spoils everything**

1) Carlson <u>stands up</u> to Curley and <u>laughs</u> at him.

2) Lennie's still <u>smiling</u> and thinking about the dream farm and the <u>rabbits</u>. Curley thinks he's <u>laughing</u> at him and he <u>attacks Lennie</u>.

3) Lennie's really scared and <u>doesn't fight back</u>.

- Lennie is compared to an <u>animal</u> again — his hands are like "<u>paws</u>". This reminds you how <u>strong</u> he is.
- Slim calls Curley a "<u>dirty little rat</u>". This shows how <u>small</u> he is compared to <u>Lennie</u>. It also makes him sound <u>sneaky</u> — Curley starts the fight <u>on purpose</u>.

Curley attacks Lennie in the bunk house.

© James Cotton

4) George orders Lennie to "<u>Get 'im</u>" — Lennie grabs Curley's fist and <u>crushes his hand</u>.

5) Slim <u>takes control</u> of the situation. He <u>tells</u> Curley to say his hand was <u>crushed in a machine</u>.

After the fight, everyone's **pretty shocked**

1) The fight shows how <u>dangerous</u> Lennie can be. Even <u>Slim</u> is <u>shocked</u> by how bad Curley's hand is.

2) It was a <u>lucky escape</u> for George and Lennie — without <u>Slim</u> they would have been <u>fired</u>.

George <u>reminds</u> everyone about what he said <u>earlier</u> — that <u>no one</u> should mess with Lennie. It's as if he <u>knew</u> something like this would <u>happen</u>.

Tension and conflict — typical Friday night if you ask me...

Lennie wouldn't fight until George told him to. At the end Lennie cries, "I didn't wanta". Lennie's just like a big kid — a really strong kid who's very violent. It makes you feel sorry for him, but also worried about what he might do next.

Analysis of Chapter Four — In Crooks's Room

Crooks, Candy and Lennie dream of a better life. Then Curley's wife comes along and spoils everything.

What happens in Chapter Four

- Lennie talks to Crooks in Crooks's room while the other men are in town.
- Candy comes in and they all talk about the dream.
- Curley's wife insults them and says their dream will never come true.

Lennie visits Crooks in his room

1) In this chapter everything happens in <u>Crooks's room</u>.
   It makes the chapter quite <u>intense</u>.

2) Crooks is rubbing "<u>liniment</u>" (medical cream) on his
   <u>aching back</u> — he has a <u>hard life</u> and is always in <u>pain</u>.

3) The other ranchers won't let Crooks in the <u>bunk house</u>.
   He tries to <u>get rid</u> of Lennie at first and is <u>mean</u> to him.

4) At first Crooks <u>can't understand</u> why George stays with Lennie.
   In the end he <u>realises</u> that it's simply "<u>bein' with another guy</u>".
   Crooks is really lonely — he doesn't have <u>anyone</u> to talk to.

© James Cotton

Crooks gets angry with Lennie.

Crooks is treated badly because he's black

1) Crooks's room is <u>completely separate</u> from the bunk house.
   He's <u>kept apart</u> from the <u>white</u> men because he's <u>black</u>.

2) Crooks's room is attached to the <u>barn</u> — he lives right <u>next</u> to the
   <u>horses</u>. This suggests that he's treated like an <u>animal</u> on the ranch.

3) Crooks cares a lot about his <u>rights</u>:

Background

When the book was written in
the <u>1930s</u>, <u>black</u> people didn't
have very many <u>rights</u>. They had
<u>separate</u> schools, hospitals and
restaurants from <u>white</u> people.

In his room there's a copy of the "<u>California civil code</u>"
— it's a book with information about <u>people's rights</u>.

Lennie, Candy and Crooks get dreaming

1) <u>Candy</u> comes in and they all talk about the <u>dream farm</u>.

2) At first Crooks doesn't think they'll <u>ever</u> get the farm.

3) Each character has <u>different hopes</u> about
   what they want to do on the farm.

4) These three characters are the <u>least powerful</u> men on
   the ranch. Crooks is <u>black and crippled</u>, Candy's <u>old</u>
   and <u>disabled</u> and Lennie's <u>not clever</u>. This suggests
   that they won't <u>be able</u> to make their dream <u>happen</u>.

Theme — Dreams

- Lennie just wants to "<u>tend the rabbits</u>".
- Candy wants land he can "<u>live on and
  there couldn't nobody throw him off it</u>".
- Crooks wants to "<u>come an' lend a hand</u>"
  for company.

Analysis of Chapter Four — In Crooks's Room

Curley's wife **breaks up** the **party**

1) The men are brought <u>back to reality</u> by <u>Curley's wife</u>. She comes in and <u>surprises</u> them.

2) She <u>looks down</u> on the three men because they're the "<u>weak ones</u>". She calls them <u>nasty names</u>.

- Crooks is a "<u>nigger</u>".
- Lennie is a "<u>dum-dum</u>".
- Candy is a "<u>lousy ol' sheep</u>".

It seems like she's getting <u>revenge</u> for all the <u>horrible things</u> the men call her — like "tart", "bitch" and "jail bait".

3) She <u>threatens Crooks</u> — "I could get you strung up on a tree so easy it ain't even funny." She means that she could pretend he <u>raped</u> her. He'd be found <u>guilty</u> and <u>hanged</u> just because he's <u>black</u>.

Theme — Prejudice

<u>Curley's wife</u> shows Crooks that his <u>position in society</u> is <u>well below</u> that of a <u>white woman</u>.

4) She makes <u>fun</u> of their dream farm. She thinks the men <u>won't</u> be able to buy the farm because they'll <u>waste</u> their money on <u>drink</u>.

She's only **mean** because she's **lonely**

1) Even though she's <u>mean</u>, Steinbeck makes the reader <u>feel sorry</u> for Curley's wife.

Theme — Dreams

Curley's wife is also <u>trapped</u> in a life that she <u>hates</u> just like the men on the ranch. She has a <u>dream</u> too — she wants to be in the "<u>pitchers</u>" (the movies).

2) She's left at <u>home</u> while her husband is visiting "Susy's place" — where the men go to visit <u>prostitutes</u>.

3) She's really <u>lonely</u> — she just wants to "<u>talk to somebody</u>".

Things go **back** to **normal**

1) When the <u>other men</u> get back, things go back to <u>normal</u> — black people and white people are <u>separated</u>.

2) The things <u>Curley's wife</u> said to Crooks have affected him <u>badly</u>. He <u>doesn't</u> want to be part of the dream any more — "I didn' mean it. Jus' foolin'."

3) Crooks returns to putting "<u>liniment</u>" on his <u>aching back</u>. This shows that Crooks's pain <u>never ends</u>.

© James Cotton

Curley's wife insults everyone in Crooks's room.

Optimism? Happiness? It can't last...

For a brief moment the dream gives Candy the confidence to stand up to Curley's wife and order her out of his room. But it doesn't last. Curley's wife puts each man in his place and crushes their dreams. She's pretty horrible really...

Analysis of Chapter Five — Lennie Kills Curley's Wife

This is the chapter where Lennie kills Curley's wife. And then gets hunted down. That's how it goes...

What happens in Chapter Five

- Lennie has accidentally killed the puppy Slim gave him.
- He talks to Curley's wife, strokes her hair and kills her by mistake.
- Lennie runs away and Curley decides to hunt him down.

Lennie's in the **barn** — he's done another **bad thing**

1) The chapter starts with a <u>peaceful</u> description of a "<u>lazy</u> and <u>warm</u>" Sunday afternoon. This contrasts with the "<u>bad thing</u>" that Lennie's done — he's <u>killed</u> his puppy.

2) Lennie's <u>angry</u> with the dead puppy because he's <u>scared</u> George won't let him tend the <u>rabbits</u> now.

Theme — Death

First Lennie killed a <u>mouse</u> and now he's killed a <u>puppy</u>. It makes you <u>wonder</u> what he'll kill <u>next</u>.

Curley's wife arrives

1) <u>Curley's wife</u> comes into the barn and <u>talks</u> to Lennie.

2) She tells Lennie that she <u>still</u> dreams of being a <u>film star</u> — "Maybe I will yet." She still hopes for a <u>better life</u>.

3) She says that she <u>married Curley</u> to "make something of myself". You <u>feel sorry</u> for her because she's <u>trapped</u> on the ranch and her <u>dreams</u> haven't come true.

© Nigel R. Barklie / Rex Features

Lennie talks to Curley's wife in the barn.

Lennie **kills** Curley's wife **by accident**

1) Curley's wife lets Lennie <u>stroke</u> her <u>soft hair</u>. He starts to stroke <u>harder</u> and she tries to <u>stop him</u>.

2) Lennie panics and becomes <u>violent</u>. He <u>holds on</u> to her and <u>shakes</u> her to get her to <u>be quiet</u>.

This is just like in <u>Weed</u> where he grabbed a girl's <u>red dress</u>. She <u>shouted</u> and he <u>panicked</u>. Lennie just "<u>holds on</u>" because it's the "<u>only thing</u>" he can think of.

3) He accidentally <u>breaks her neck</u> because he's so strong.

4) Lennie is <u>confused</u> and <u>panicked</u>. This is shown by the <u>different emotions</u> he goes through:

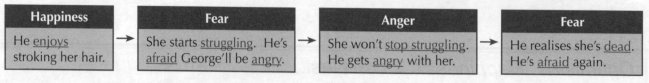

Happiness	Fear	Anger	Fear
He <u>enjoys</u> stroking her hair.	She starts <u>struggling</u>. He's <u>afraid</u> George'll be <u>angry</u>.	She won't <u>stop struggling</u>. He gets <u>angry</u> with her.	He realises she's <u>dead</u>. He's <u>afraid</u> again.

Analysis of Chapter Five — Lennie Kills Curley's Wife

Now *everyone's dreams* are *over*

1) Lennie's actions mean that <u>George's dream</u> of owning his own <u>land</u> is <u>over</u>. He knows he'll end up spending his monthly wages on <u>women</u> and <u>whisky</u> just like the other ranch workers.

2) Candy's <u>worried</u> about what will happen to <u>Lennie</u> — he says Lennie is "such a <u>nice fella</u>" and a "poor bastard". He thinks that Curley will <u>find</u> him and <u>kill</u> him.

Character — Candy

It's Candy's "<u>greatest fear</u>" that the dream is <u>over</u>. This shows <u>how much</u> it means to him.

3) Candy <u>blames</u> Curley's wife for <u>ruining the dream</u>. He shouts at her body — "Ever'body knowed you'd <u>mess things up</u>." This might sound <u>selfish</u> because she's been killed, but it shows that he's <u>really upset</u> about what's happened.

Curley wants *revenge*

1) Curley doesn't even <u>touch</u> his dead <u>wife</u>. This shows how <u>horrible</u> and <u>uncaring</u> he is.

2) It's <u>Slim</u> who checks whether Curley's wife is <u>dead</u>. He goes to her "<u>quietly</u>" and touches her <u>gently</u>.

3) His <u>calm</u> actions are the <u>opposite</u> of Curley's "<u>fury</u>".

Character — Curley

Curley cares more about getting his <u>own back</u> than losing his wife. He sees her death as a chance to <u>get</u> Lennie.

4) <u>Slim</u> suggests to Curley that he should "<u>stay here with your wife</u>" but Curley wants to <u>fight</u>. He wants <u>revenge</u> for her death, and for his <u>crushed hand</u>.

Slim and Curley realise that Curley's wife is dead.

© James Cotton

George *plans to* kill Lennie

1) George <u>knows</u> he has to find Lennie <u>before</u> Curley and the men do or they'll kill him <u>painfully</u>. He isn't going to "<u>let 'em hurt Lennie</u>".

2) Carlson <u>can't find</u> his gun. George "<u>weakly</u>" suggests that Carlson's <u>lost</u> it. This gives you a clue that George might have <u>taken</u> the gun to shoot Lennie <u>himself</u>.

- George hopes that Lennie could just be <u>locked up</u> instead of <u>killed</u>.

- Slim says that they would "<u>strap him down</u>" and put him in a "<u>cage</u>".

- Slim knows that it would be <u>better</u> for Lennie to be killed by <u>George</u> rather than Curley.

Don't ask Lennie for directions — he'll lead you to a dead end...

Curley's wife has a rough time in this novel. We find out that she's not really a horrible tart — she's just a lonely girl who dreams of being a movie star. And then she gets killed. We never even find out her name. It's all very sad...

Analysis of Chapter Six — George Shoots Lennie

The story ends by the pool where it started. Lennie's scared of what he's done and waits for George.

What happens in Chapter Six

- Lennie hides by the pool where he stayed with George in Chapter One.
- George finds him and tells him about the dream again.
- As the men get closer, George shoots Lennie.

Lennie goes **back** to the **pool**

1) Lennie <u>returns</u> to the spot where George told him to hide if he got into <u>trouble</u> again.

2) The pool is linked to <u>death</u>.

Theme — Destiny

Lennie's <u>return</u> to this hiding place makes it seem like his <u>destiny</u> was <u>already decided</u>. George <u>knew</u> that Lennie would need a place to <u>hide</u>.

It's where George threw away Lennie's <u>dead mouse</u> in Chapter One. → It's where a <u>heron</u> eats a <u>water snake</u> in this chapter. → This suggests that <u>Lennie</u> will be <u>killed</u> here.

He feels **guilty** — he **remembers** being **told off** in the past

Lennie hides by the pool.

© James Cotton

1) Lennie knows he's done a "<u>bad thing</u>".

2) He has <u>visions</u> of his Aunt Clara and a giant rabbit.

3) The two characters are Lennie's <u>conscience</u>. They <u>tell him off</u> for all the bad things he's done.

4) Lennie doesn't feel <u>guilty</u> about killing Curley's wife. He <u>only</u> feels guilty about <u>letting George down</u>.

5) He <u>worries</u> that he won't be able to tend the <u>rabbits</u>.

The **giant rabbit** upsets Lennie

1) The rabbit's <u>language</u> is <u>similar</u> to <u>George's</u> when he's <u>angry</u> with Lennie. The rabbit calls Lennie a "<u>crazy bastard</u>" and it says that George will "<u>go away an' leave you</u>". This shows that Lennie's <u>greatest fear</u> is that George will get <u>fed up</u> with him and leave.

2) The things that Aunt Clara and the rabbit say <u>suggest</u> that Lennie is beginning to <u>understand</u> that what he's done has <u>destroyed</u> his and George's <u>dream</u>.

3) George <u>finds Lennie</u> while the rabbit is <u>upsetting him</u>. This is when Lennie <u>needs</u> him the <u>most</u>.

The fact that Lennie <u>imagines</u> talking to his Aunt Clara and a giant rabbit shows how <u>scared</u> and <u>confused</u> his guilt has made him.

Analysis of Chapter Six — George Shoots Lennie

George won't let **anyone else** kill Lennie

1) George <u>knows</u> he has to <u>kill Lennie</u>:

George doesn't want to kill Lennie...	**...but he knows he has no choice.**
• Lennie's his <u>only friend</u>. They've <u>known</u> each other for <u>years</u>. • His life would have <u>no meaning</u> without Lennie to <u>look after</u> — he'd just be another <u>lonely</u> ranch worker.	• If <u>Curley</u> catches Lennie, he'll <u>kill</u> him in a really <u>painful</u> way. • If Curley <u>doesn't</u> catch him, Lennie will <u>starve</u> to <u>death</u>. He wouldn't be able to cope <u>without George</u>.

2) <u>Candy</u> let <u>Carlson</u> shoot his dog, but George won't let <u>anyone else</u> kill Lennie.

3) He takes <u>responsibility</u> for killing Lennie because he <u>cares</u> about him.

George finds it hard to shoot **Lennie**

1) George uses the <u>dream</u> to <u>distract</u> Lennie so that he can shoot him from <u>behind</u>.

2) George finds it really <u>difficult</u> to shoot Lennie because he <u>cares</u> about him:

• He speaks "<u>shakily</u>" as if he's nervous.

• His hand "<u>shook violently</u>" as he holds the gun.

• After shooting Lennie he <u>throws away</u> the gun.

© Ben Franske

George gets ready to shoot Lennie.

The characters **react differently** to Lennie's death

Curley   He's <u>impressed</u> that George shot him "Right in the <u>back of the head</u>".

George   He's in <u>shock</u> over what's happened. He can <u>hardly speak</u>.

Slim   He <u>comforts George</u> — "I swear you hadda."

Carlson   He <u>can't understand</u> why George and Slim are so <u>depressed</u>.

I met an angry giant rabbit once — he was hopping mad...

Not the best joke ever — but try lightening the mood after all that. The story ends where it all began, only I'm more depressed than I was at the start of the book. Anyway I won't keep rabbiting on (I'm sorry...) — let's meet the characters.

Practice Questions

Well, that's what happens in *Of Mice and Men*. Have a go at these questions to check how much you've remembered and understood. Just answer each one with a few words or a sentence.

Quick Questions

Q1 Give an example of an animal that Lennie is compared to in Chapter One.

Q2 What part of the dream does Lennie get most excited about?

Q3 Why does George tell Lennie to remember the place by the pool?

Q4 What colour does Curley's wife wear a lot of?

Q5 Why does Carlson hate Candy's dog?

Q6 What does Candy offer to George and Lennie that will help their dream to come true?

Q7 Why does Crooks live in a separate building from the other ranchers?

Q8 Who interrupts Crooks, Candy and Lennie talking about the dream?

Practice Questions

Here are a few more quick questions to test your knowledge of the novel's events. There are also some in-depth questions which will help with your revision. You need to write a paragraph for each of these.

Quick Questions

Q9   What is Curley's wife's dream?

Q10   How does Candy feel about Curley's wife after Lennie has killed her?
a)   He's angry with her for spoiling their dreams.
b)   He's upset because he liked her a lot.
c)   He's scared because he might get the blame.

Q11   In Chapter Six, Lennie sees a vision of his Aunt Clara. What else does he see a vision of?

Q12   Which character comforts George after he's killed Lennie?

In-depth Questions

Q1   Which events help the reader to get an impression of George and Lennie's relationship?

Q2   Which character do you feel most sympathy for in the novel and why?

Q3   Does Steinbeck show any of the characters changing as the novel goes on?
Explain why you think this.

Q4   Which details give the reader the strongest impression of what life was like for ranch hands in the 1930s?

Character Profile — George

Slim says not many people do what George does — team up with a friend to work on the ranches. You've got to admire him for looking after Lennie. But he doesn't get a happy ending — he has to kill his best friend.

George is **loyal** to Lennie

1) George and Lennie are <u>friends</u>. They travel together looking for <u>work</u>.

2) George <u>looks after</u> Lennie:

> - He tells Lennie <u>what to do</u> and how to <u>behave</u>.
> - He gets Lennie <u>out of trouble</u> — like in Weed.
> - He makes sure Lennie has <u>food</u> and a <u>job</u>.
> - Even when he kills Lennie, he tries to be as <u>gentle</u> as possible.

3) He <u>doesn't</u> always treat Lennie well. He once told him to <u>jump into a river</u>. He often <u>shouts</u> at him and calls him a "crazy bastard", but he's <u>ashamed</u> of that now.

George has **no problems** when he's **on his own**

1) George is <u>quite smart</u> — he manages to find work for him and Lennie.

2) When he gets <u>angry</u>, he <u>often</u> says he'd be better off <u>alone</u> — "if I was alone <u>I could live so easy</u>".

3) George isn't <u>just</u> with Lennie because he feels he has to. Lennie is his friend and lets George <u>believe</u> that the <u>dream</u> of owning a farm could come true.

George is...

loyal: "I want you to stay with me, Lennie."

grumpy: "You crazy fool."

caring: "I ain't gonna let 'em hurt Lennie."

George is a **realistic character**

1) George is a <u>normal</u> guy — he <u>enjoys</u> things that most people would enjoy like <u>being free</u> from work or being his <u>own boss</u>.

2) Sometimes the reader <u>feels sorry</u> for George — Lennie makes life <u>hard</u> for him.

3) George gets <u>frustrated</u> with Lennie and shouts at him. This makes him a <u>realistic</u> character — a lot of people would <u>lose patience</u> in his situation.

Writer's Techniques

George is the <u>hero</u> of *Of Mice and Men*, but he's just an <u>ordinary</u> man. This makes it <u>easier</u> for the reader to <u>understand</u> why he does things.

George is a good man but he has flaws.

© Moviestore Collection Ltd / Alamy

Character Profile — George

George can get **angry**

1) When <u>Candy</u> wants to join their dream farm, George gets <u>angry</u> — "You got nothing to do with us."

2) He tells Lennie to <u>fight back</u> against Curley — even though it could get them into <u>trouble</u>.

3) When Slim says it's <u>unusual</u> that George and Lennie travel together, George <u>snaps</u> at him.

4) He's mean to <u>Lennie</u> when he's <u>frustrated</u> at him.

Theme — Loneliness

George says lonely men "<u>get mean</u>" and want to "<u>fight all the time</u>". George's <u>anger</u> suggests he <u>could</u> be like that too. His friendship with <u>Lennie</u> seems to be the <u>only</u> thing <u>stopping</u> him from getting into fights.

George gets angry with Curley.

© Mikki Schaffner

He's good at **understanding people**

1) George is good at knowing when people can be <u>trusted</u> or when they might <u>cause trouble</u> for him and Lennie.

Writer's Techniques

George <u>senses</u> that something <u>bad</u> is going to happen at the ranch. He thinks it isn't a <u>good place</u> to be — "I don't like it". This builds the <u>suspense</u> for the reader.

2) George wants to <u>avoid</u> Curley because he's <u>mean</u>. He's scared he's "gonna <u>tangle</u> with that bastard".

3) He doesn't like Curley's wife either — he thinks she'll cause <u>trouble</u>.

4) However, he <u>likes</u> Slim and tells him what happened in Weed — he knows he's <u>trustworthy</u>.

The **dream** keeps him **going**

1) George isn't <u>in control</u> of his own life. He has to work for people he <u>doesn't respect</u>, like Curley. He also can't control Lennie's <u>unpredictable</u> behaviour.

Theme — Destiny

For George the <u>dream</u> is about being in charge of his <u>own destiny</u>. He's <u>tired</u> of drifting through life.

2) George talks about the dream farm to keep Lennie <u>happy</u>. Sometimes he gets so involved in it that he believes it himself. In Chapter Three he's "<u>entranced</u>" (put under a spell) by the thought of it.

3) In the end George is <u>free</u> to "<u>live so easy</u>" without Lennie. Steinbeck makes it clear that Lennie's death isn't a <u>happy ending</u> for George — he'll be <u>lonely</u> without his friend.

George has got some issues...

At first George seems really normal, but he's carrying a lot of emotional baggage. He's often quite depressed, he's very defensive and he has a low opinion of most people. His short fuse isn't that surprising though — Lennie's quite a handful.

Character Profile — Lennie

Lennie's a likeable, even lovable character. He likes the simple things in life — fluffy animals and ketchup. He's not harmless though and it's his destructive side that gets him and George into trouble.

Lennie is a huge, grown man — but also very **childlike**

1) He's <u>powerful</u> with <u>huge hands</u> — this makes him a <u>brilliant</u> worker.

Lennie is...

childlike: "He's jes' like a kid".

strong: "Strong as a bull."

like an animal: "snorting into the water like a horse".

2) He's got a <u>grown-up's body</u> but has the <u>mind of a child</u>.

3) Lennie's condition is <u>never explained</u>. He's called a "<u>dum-dum</u>" but George says that he "ain't no cuckoo".

4) Lennie asks lots of <u>innocent questions</u> — "Where we goin', George?" Slim sees that Lennie "<u>ain't mean</u>".

5) He likes to stroke <u>soft</u> things like mice and Curley's wife's hair. He's like a <u>child</u> with a <u>favourite stuffed toy</u>.

He's compared to **animals** a lot

1) He looks <u>like a bear</u> and walks like a bear that "drags his paws".

2) He eats and drinks like a <u>hungry animal</u>.

3) He <u>never</u> wants to let animals out of his <u>sight</u> like the puppies in the barn or the dead mouse at the pool.

Language

Comparing Lennie to a bear shows that he's <u>powerful</u> but he's <u>not very bright</u>.

4) Lennie's a bit like <u>George's pet</u>:

- He <u>follows</u> George around and <u>relies</u> on him for food.

- He <u>obeys</u> George — he brings George the mouse "like a <u>terrier</u>".

He **depends** on George

1) George has <u>looked after</u> Lennie since Lennie's Aunt Clara died. Lennie <u>couldn't have survived</u> on his own.

2) Lennie is a <u>good worker</u> though. Slim says, "nobody can keep up with him". This is <u>useful</u> for George because it helps them get <u>work</u>.

3) George and Lennie are a good <u>team</u>. George has the <u>brains</u> and Lennie has the <u>strength</u>.

Lennie's surname is "Small". This is ironic, because he's "a huge man". Irony is when you say something but you mean the opposite.

Lennie likes to stroke animals.

Character Profile — Lennie

Lennie has **moments** of **cunning**

1) He knows that George would feel guilty about leaving him. He uses this to his advantage to get George to tell him about their dream farm.

2) He realises George does a lot for him. When he has the imaginary conversation with his Aunt Clara she says that George does nice things for him "alla time". It shows that he's aware that George makes sacrifices for him.

Lennie sits in the barn.

© Ben Franske

Lennie's a **killer**...

1) Lennie is the gentlest character in the novel but he's also the most destructive.

Theme — Destiny

Lennie's violence gets worse throughout the novel. This makes the reader think that he'll seriously hurt someone someday.

2) He can be dangerous and violent. He attacks Curley and Curley's wife, kills mice and throws his dead puppy across the barn.

3) Lennie holds onto Curley's wife because he's scared. When she starts struggling against him Lennie's "in a panic", and he cries "with fright".

4) Lennie's fear tends to turn into anger — Steinbeck tells us twice that Lennie is "angry" with Curley's wife. He's so angry that he shakes her to death.

...but the reader **feels sorry** for him

Steinbeck makes the reader feel that it's not Lennie's fault when he hurts animals and people:

- It's George who tells him to "get" Curley.

- He kills the animals and Curley's wife because he can't control his own strength.

- When Curley attacked Lennie he was "jus' scairt", and he didn't know what to do.

- In Weed, Lennie held on to the girl's dress because "that's the only thing he can think to do".

Slim says Lennie "ain't a bit mean". Slim's the wisest character in the novel so this makes the reader think that Lennie doesn't hurt anything or anyone on purpose.

Lennie's harmless, he wouldn't hurt a... err...

Lennie isn't a bad man — he just has trouble controlling himself. He's capable of showing kindness, in his own way — when they talk about ketchup he says, "But I wouldn't eat none, George. I'd leave it all for you." That's true friendship.

Character Profile — Slim

Slim is respected on the ranch. All the other characters listen to him and take his advice. Despite his power, Slim can't stop the sad events of the story from happening.

Slim is an **excellent** worker

1) He's a "jerkline skinner" which means he controls a team of mules — a very skilled job. He's easy-going and good to work for.

2) He's described as "the prince of the ranch" and he has "authority".

3) Slim's fit and healthy. He's tall and elegant like his name.

Slim is...

respected: "his word was taken on any subject".
mysterious: "understanding beyond thought".
Godlike: "calm, Godlike eyes".

Slim helps people in **practical ways**

- He thinks that Candy's dog should be killed. He's not being cruel — it's practical. The dog was old and was suffering.

- He organises Curley's trip to the doctor when Lennie breaks his hand.

- He says Lennie has to be killed at the end — "I guess we gotta get 'im".

- Slim comforts George after he's shot Lennie — he sits next to him, then takes him off for a drink.

Slim is practical but he's also sympathetic. He understands why George is so upset about Lennie.

Slim is the **spiritual** leader of the men

1) Slim has a strong sense of right and wrong. People listen to him and trust his opinions.

2) He understands that weak people or animals are less likely to survive. He could have stopped Candy's dog being killed by Carlson, but he chose not to.

3) The language Steinbeck uses to describe Slim shows that he's different from the other characters. Steinbeck writes that Slim "moved with a majesty", and he "heard more than was said to him". This makes him seem quite spiritual.

Theme — Prejudice

Slim calls Crooks by his name instead of "nigger" or "stable buck". He treats him with more respect than the other characters.

© James Cotton

Slim is liked and respected.

Slim's the ranch's God, or something like that...

Slim's a pretty brave and fearless guy. When Curley picks a fight with Lennie, Slim tries to step in — "I'll get 'um myself." Unlike the other guys, he's not afraid of Curley and would risk losing his job to protect Lennie. What a hero.

Character Profile — Crooks

Crooks has suffered and been treated differently because he's black. He may not appear much in the book but he says some important things. In fact, the whole of Chapter Four is set in his room.

Only **Crooks** has his **own room**

1) Crooks's room is <u>small</u> and <u>basic</u>. It's <u>homely</u> and it's <u>his own</u> — it's full of his <u>belongings</u>.

2) He owns rubber boots, an alarm clock and a shotgun which shows that he's <u>practical</u> and <u>active</u>. His books show that he <u>reads</u> and <u>thinks</u> too.

3) He snaps at people when they try to come into his room — "You got no right to come in my room." <u>Privacy</u> is one of the few <u>rights</u> he has.

Crooks is...

proud: "a proud, aloof man".

cynical: "nobody gets no land".

defenceless: Curley's wife says, "I could get you strung up on a tree so easy".

Theme — Loneliness

Crooks <u>pretends</u> his <u>loneliness</u> doesn't affect him, but Steinbeck makes it clear that it <u>does</u>.

Crooks is a **victim** of **racism**

Racism is treating somebody unfairly because of their race.

1) Crooks is the <u>only black man</u> in the book. He's not allowed in the bunk house because of his <u>colour</u> — the other workers say it's because he <u>smells</u>.

Theme — Prejudice

Steinbeck is <u>showing</u> how black people were <u>usually treated</u> in America in the <u>1930s</u>.

2) He's <u>lonely</u> — he says, "A guy needs somebody".

3) His loneliness makes him <u>jealous</u> of George and Lennie's <u>friendship</u>. In Chapter Four he tries to make Lennie feel as <u>lonely</u> as he does by saying that George might <u>leave</u> him.

He doesn't have much **power**

1) Crooks is <u>really good</u> at his job but he's the <u>least important</u> of the ranch workers.

2) He offers to work on the dream farm for <u>free</u>. This is because life on the farm would give him something to be <u>proud</u> of, which he doesn't have now.

3) When Crooks <u>stands up</u> to Curley's wife she threatens to have him hung. He knows he has <u>no power</u> so he tries to make himself <u>invisible</u> — he "reduced himself to nothing".

Crooks and Lennie in Crooks's room.

Another depressing story... whatever next...

Crooks thinks the ranch hands' dream will never happen. He's seen too many men "with land in their head" that are just kidding themselves — he knows they'll end up spending their money on either women or whisky. Jolly.

Character Profile — Candy

Candy's story is almost as depressing as Lennie's. He's a victim of a life of work. He's already lost a hand, and during the story he loses his dog and his dream. At the end he lays down and covers his eyes.

Candy *seems harmless* — but he can be *mean*

1) He <u>makes friends</u> with Lennie and George — the dream farm <u>brings them together</u>.

2) He <u>feels sorry</u> for Lennie after he kills Curley's wife — he calls him a "Poor bastard".

3) He's not always <u>nice</u> to people though. He <u>blames</u> Curley's wife for her own death. He <u>shouts</u> at her body and calls her a "<u>God damn tramp</u>". It shows how <u>upset</u> he is that his plans are <u>spoiled</u>.

Candy is...

old: "stoop shouldered old man".

weak: "I wisht somebody'd shoot me".

one-handed: "I ain't much good with on'y one hand."

He's *frail* and *powerless* — like his *dog*

© James Cotton

Candy is upset when Carlson kills his dog.

1) Candy is <u>weak</u> and <u>disabled</u> — he lost his right hand in a machine on the farm.

2) Candy is <u>old</u> and <u>useless</u> like his dog. He's worried that he'll face the <u>same fate</u>.

3) He's <u>not</u> respected by the others:

- He's the "swamper" (cleaner). It's one of the <u>least respected jobs</u> on the ranch.

- <u>No one</u> tries to save his dog from <u>being shot</u>.

- He's always getting <u>left behind</u> — he doesn't go with the men when they go into <u>town</u>.

Theme — Prejudice

Candy suffers <u>prejudice</u> because of his <u>age</u> and his <u>disability</u>.

He's wants a *better life*

1) Candy is very <u>quick</u> to get involved with George and Lennie's <u>dream</u> — he offers them <u>all</u> of his <u>money</u> even though he's only known them for <u>one day</u>.

2) Candy offers to help <u>pay</u> for the ranch because he wants a share of his <u>own land</u> — "I'll be on our own place". This is his version of the American Dream (see p.8).

3) Joining in George and Lennie's plan for a farm of their own gives him some <u>self-respect</u>.

Lots of people in America wanted to work for themselves. This was their American Dream.

Poor Candy — he doesn't have any mates that'll shoot him...

It's a bit odd that Candy offers George and Lennie all his money — they've only just met. It shows just how desperate he is to get off the ranch and have a little bit of land to call his own. It's a shame it all comes to nothing in the end...

Character Profile — Carlson and Whit

Carlson and Whit are more minor characters. Carlson is heartless — he convinces Candy to let him shoot his dog. Whit is young and lively — he likes the simple things in life.

Carlson is Mr Insensitive

1) Carlson doesn't think about other people's <u>feelings</u>.

- He thinks Candy's dog should be <u>shot</u> because it's old and smelly. He can't see that Candy might <u>love</u> his dog.

- He <u>doesn't apologise</u> for shooting Candy's dog. He <u>cleans his gun</u> in front of Candy — he <u>doesn't care</u> about his feelings.

- He <u>doesn't understand</u> why George and Slim seem <u>upset</u> at the end of the novel. He doesn't feel <u>sorry</u> about Lennie's death.

> **Carlson is...**
>
> **violent:** "I'll kick your God damn head off".
>
> **insensitive:** "what the hell ya suppose is eatin' them two guys?"

2) He's <u>quick to pick a fight</u> with Curley. He calls him "yella as a frog belly" and a "<u>God damn punk</u>". This shows that he's got a <u>quick temper</u>.

Whit is fun but he's lonely

1) Whit's a <u>fun</u> guy — he's <u>not bitter</u> about ranch life. The <u>reader</u> knows he'll probably end up <u>sad</u> and <u>lonely</u>, but he doesn't seem <u>aware</u> of this.

2) Whit plays <u>cards</u> with George, but as soon as they get <u>talking</u>, he's "<u>not interested</u>" in the game. He's more interested in being George's <u>friend</u>.

> **Whit is...**
>
> **young:** "A young laboring man".
>
> **fun-loving:** "a guy got to have some fun sometime".

He's doomed to stay on the ranch

In some ways Whit's already been <u>affected</u> by the <u>hard life on the ranch</u>.

- Life seems to be <u>weighing</u> him down as if he's carrying an "<u>invisible grain bag</u>".

- He's <u>sad</u> and <u>misses</u> his friend <u>Bill Tenner</u>.

- He goes to "old Susy's" <u>brothel</u> and <u>wastes</u> his money on <u>girls</u> and <u>drink</u>. He has no <u>ambition</u>.

> **Theme — Destiny**
>
> Whit <u>represents</u> what <u>George</u> could become <u>without Lennie</u> and their dream farm.

Whit plays the guitar, Slim reads a magazine and Candy sits with his dog.

© Mikki Schaffner

Whit's doomed too — what, you couldn't see it coming...

You can't just forget about Carlson and Whit. They're both typical ranch hands and their loneliness shows how important friendship is. Carlson also shoots Candy's dog and he provokes Curley before the hand-crushing incident.

Character Profile — Curley

Curley's the only proper bad guy on the ranch and he's the only one who deserves what happens to him.

No one likes Curley

1) It seems like Curley's in a <u>strong position</u> on the ranch. He's young, fit and healthy. He's the <u>boss's son</u> and he's just <u>married</u> an attractive woman.

2) However, no one respects him — so he's probably quite <u>lonely</u>.

3) He wears "<u>high-heeled boots</u>". These give him extra <u>height</u> because he's "<u>little</u>". They also show he's in charge — they make it clear that he's "<u>not a laboring man</u>".

Theme — Destiny

Curley's <u>trapped</u> on <u>the ranch</u> just like the others. Because he's the <u>boss's son</u>, he's <u>destined</u> to run it himself one day.

Curley is mean and aggressive.

© Ben Franske

Curley likes to **pick fights**

1) Candy calls Curley "<u>handy</u>" — meaning he <u>fights well</u>. <u>Fighting</u> is the one thing he's <u>good</u> at, and he likes to show off his <u>skills</u>.

Curley is...

insecure: "You seen a girl around here?"
aggressive: "He's alla time picking scraps".
disliked: "This guy Curley sounds like a son-of-a-bitch to me."

Theme — Loneliness

Curley's just as <u>lonely</u> as the other characters. None of the <u>bunk house men</u> like him, and neither does his <u>wife</u>.

2) He's <u>angry</u> about being <u>short</u>. He uses violence to make up for it. He picks fights to try and <u>prove</u> something, but it just makes the men <u>dislike</u> him more.

3) Curley's an <u>outsider</u> — he's <u>not</u> one of the bunk house men. He <u>wants attention</u> and <u>respect</u>.

Curley isn't **happily married**

1) Curley's wife <u>married</u> him as a way of <u>getting away</u> from her old life. She admits that "He ain't a nice fella."

2) Curley and his wife only appear <u>together</u> when she's <u>dead</u>. He doesn't <u>touch</u> her even then — it's Slim who checks to see if she's <u>really dead</u>.

3) Curley wants to <u>kill Lennie</u> instead of staying with his wife. He doesn't really <u>care</u> about her — he's just <u>angry</u> that Lennie has taken away something <u>belonging</u> to him.

Theme — Women

Curley doesn't <u>understand</u> what his wife <u>needs</u> from him — <u>company</u> and <u>attention</u>.

If you beat up everyone in sight, you probably won't have any friends...

Don't feel too sorry for Curley — he's still a punk. Curley is an example of what George says about lonely people — they get "mean". Curley wants attention, just like his wife, but instead of flirting he gets all angry. The big baby...

Character Profile — Curley's Wife

Curley's wife is the only woman we actually meet in the book. In some ways she seems bold and confident, but in other ways she's very fragile. One thing's for sure — she's not happy.

The **men** have **lots** to say about **Curley's wife**

1) The men <u>worry</u> about Curley's wife because she's so <u>flirty</u>. They know if they flirt back, Curley would start a fight and they'd probably <u>lose their jobs</u>.

2) The men <u>aren't nice</u> to her but she doesn't leave them alone — she <u>bursts</u> into the bunk house <u>all the time</u>.

3) The men call her "<u>jail bait</u>" and a "<u>rattrap</u>". This shows that she's seen as a <u>threat</u> who causes <u>trouble</u>.

Steinbeck doesn't give Curley's wife a name to show that she belongs to Curley.

© Ben Franske

Curley's wife is unhappy and lonely.

She's very **attractive**

1) She's "<u>purty</u>". She wears lots of <u>make-up</u> and uses her looks to get <u>attention</u>.

2) Lennie is <u>fascinated</u> by her. She is another <u>soft</u> thing that he wants to <u>touch</u>.

3) She wears a lot of <u>red</u> — her lips are "<u>rouged</u>" and her fingernails and shoes are red. This links her to the <u>girl in Weed</u> with the <u>red dress</u> — it's a <u>hint</u> that Lennie will <u>hurt</u> Curley's wife, too.

Curley's wife is...

pretty: "She's purty".

lonely: "I get awful lonely."

flirty: "She got the eye goin' all the time".

Curley's wife is described as having curls like "<u>sausages</u>" and a "<u>rouged</u>" face — she wears too much make-up and looks <u>false</u> and <u>harsh</u>. When she's dead, she's "<u>pretty and simple</u>". Steinbeck is showing that her <u>hard life</u> made her mean, but after death she looks <u>innocent</u> again.

She isn't happy on the **ranch**

1) Curley's wife is <u>lonely</u>.

2) When she <u>pretends</u> to be looking for Curley she's really looking for <u>attention</u> from the men.

- She's the <u>only woman</u> on the ranch.
- The men <u>don't want</u> to <u>talk</u> to her.
- Her husband <u>doesn't spend</u> any <u>time</u> with her.

3) She says, "Think I don't like to talk to somebody ever' once in a while?" This makes us <u>feel sorry</u> for her.

4) She wanted to be a <u>movie star</u>, but she never made it. She <u>escaped</u> from her <u>controlling</u> mother but ended up being controlled by Curley instead. This was what life was like for some <u>women</u> in the <u>1930s</u>.

Most of the men hate her but she doesn't really deserve it...

Curley's wife doesn't actually get involved with any of the men — even though everyone keeps saying that she's a tart and a flirt. She's just lonely and fed up with her husband. You would be too — "Glove fulla vaseline". Eww...

Practice Questions

Well, they certainly are a cheery lot, aren't they? What with killing dogs, getting into fights and generally being miserable — living on a ranch doesn't seem like a laugh a minute. More like one a year... Anyway, miserable or not, you need to know enough about the characters to answer the questions on the next two pages. The quick questions on this page just need a word or two or a short sentence for each answer.

Quick Questions

Q1   Give two examples of the way George looks after Lennie.

Q2   Write down two words that describe what Lennie is like.

Q3   Which of these words best describes Slim:
a) cunning   b) practical   c) a gossip?

Q4   Say which of the following best describes Crooks:
a) He's arrogant and doesn't like other people.
b) He's really lonely and secretly longs for friendship.

Q5   Write one sentence describing Candy.

Q6   Write a sentence describing how Curley's wife behaves on the ranch.

Practice Questions

Here's a lovely set of in-depth and exam-style questions for you to have a go at. The in-depth questions only need quite short answers — about a paragraph long. For the exam-style questions you need to write full essay answers — no fobbing me off with one-sentence answers. Don't try to do them all at once though.

In-depth Questions

Q1   Do you think that George likes having Lennie around? Why / Why not?

Q2   Who is more respected on the ranch — Slim or Curley?
Explain your choice with some quotes.

Q3   Do you feel sorry for Curley's wife? Why / Why not?

Exam-style Questions

Q1 a)   Re-read the passage in Chapter Two which begins "A tall man stood in the doorway." and ends with, "'You the new guys?'".

How does Steinbeck use details in this passage to give the reader an impression of Slim?

Think about:
• What Slim says and does.
• How he is described.

  b)   How does the rest of the novel support this impression of him?

Q2 a)   Look again at the passage in Chapter One from "'Well, we ain't got any,'" to "'I wisht I could put you in a cage with about a million mice an' let you have fun.'"

How is the character of George presented in this extract?

Think about:
• What he says and does.
• His relationship with Lennie.

  b)   How does Steinbeck present the character of George through his relationship with other characters in the rest of the novel?

Loneliness

I think loneliness is a really big theme in *Of Mice and Men*. Steinbeck gave us a hint that it's pretty important by calling the town near the ranch "Soledad". This means 'solitude' or 'loneliness' in Spanish (Ooooooh...).

Everyone on the ranch is *lonely*

The men on the ranch have "<u>no family</u>" — they're all lonely.

Slim: "Maybe ever'body in the whole damn world is scared of each other."

Ranchers
George says <u>ranchers</u> are the "<u>loneliest</u> guys in the world." It's <u>unusual</u> for the ranchers to travel <u>together</u> like George and Lennie.

Crooks
Crooks, the stable hand, lives <u>separately</u> from the others because he's <u>black</u>. He says, "a guy gets <u>too lonely</u> an' he gets <u>sick</u>". Crooks is <u>used</u> to being <u>lonely</u> on the ranch.

Curley
Curley's <u>lonely</u> even though he's <u>married</u>. The only time we see him with his wife is when she's <u>dead</u>. <u>Curley's wife</u> gets "<u>awful lonely</u>" because she's supposed to stay in the house "<u>alla time</u>".

Lennie and Crooks talk in Crooks's room.

1) Even <u>marriage</u> doesn't stop people from being lonely.

2) <u>Loneliness</u> isn't something the characters can <u>change</u>.

Looking for *companionship* can end *badly*

1) When <u>anyone</u> tries to find <u>friendship</u> it ends in <u>disaster</u>:

- <u>George</u> and <u>Lennie</u> give each other <u>companionship</u>.

- <u>George</u> still ends up just like the <u>other ranchers</u>. At the end of the novel he's <u>lonely</u> and has <u>no dreams</u>.

2) Curley's wife tries to find <u>companionship</u> by flirting with the ranchers. The men on the ranch seem <u>uncomfortable</u> and <u>don't</u> flirt back. It's her <u>flirting</u> with <u>Lennie</u> that leads to her <u>death</u>.

3) <u>Animals</u> provide a <u>temporary solution</u> to the problem of <u>loneliness</u>, but it <u>doesn't last</u>. Lennie <u>kills</u> all the animals he gets, like the mouse and the puppy. Candy has his dog until Carlson <u>shoots it</u>.

Lennie and George at the pool.

I'd be lonely if I lived and worked in the middle of nowhere...

Hmmm, living in the countryside, far away from any big towns, seeing the same people every single day and working really, really hard all the time. It just sounds awful. I'm so glad my life is nothing like that. Nothing at all... Oh dear.

Prejudice

Prejudice is a major theme in *Of Mice and Men*. In the novel, Crooks and Candy are the characters who have to put up with the most prejudice on the ranch. This is because Crooks is black, and Candy is old and disabled.

There's a lot of **prejudice** in 'Of Mice and Men'

> Prejudice means having a <u>negative opinion</u> of someone because of things like their <u>age</u> or <u>race</u>. People get <u>judged</u> based on these things <u>instead</u> of what they're <u>actually like</u>. People are often <u>treated badly</u> because others are <u>prejudiced against them</u>.

There was a lot of <u>prejudice</u> in America in the <u>1930s</u>.

1) <u>Black people</u> were <u>separated</u> from white people in schools, prisons and hospitals (see p.7).

2) <u>Farm work</u> was very <u>physical</u> and you needed to be <u>fit</u> to do it. It was really hard to get a job if you were <u>old</u> or <u>disabled</u>.

Women also experienced a lot of prejudice in the 1930s. See p.38.

Crooks is treated **badly** because of his **race**

1) Crooks <u>lives separately</u> from the other men. He's <u>ignored</u> and <u>picked on</u> by the other workers. At Christmas one of them <u>started a fight</u> with him for <u>no reason</u>.

Key Quote

Crooks: "If I say something, why it's just a nigger sayin' it."

2) Crooks is <u>picked on</u> by the boss all the time — he's always giving Crooks "<u>hell</u>". Crooks is an <u>easy target</u> because he's <u>black</u>.

3) Crooks <u>likes</u> the idea of the <u>dream farm</u> because he believes that he'll be treated like an <u>equal</u> there. He's the <u>first</u> one to <u>realise</u> that the dream <u>isn't possible</u> though — he's used to disappointment.

© James Cotton

Crooks reads alone in his room.

Candy is treated **badly** because of his **age** and **disability**

1) Candy is <u>old</u> and knows it won't be long before they "<u>can</u>" (fire) him from his job. After that, he won't be able to <u>get a job</u> because he's <u>old</u> and has <u>lost one hand</u>.

Theme — Dreams

Candy wants to be part of the <u>dream farm</u>. He'll be able to <u>keep working</u> even when he "ain't no good at it".

Key Quote

Candy: "I ain't much good with on'y one hand."

2) Candy's <u>feelings</u> don't seem to be very <u>important</u> to the men on the ranch. He doesn't get much <u>sympathy</u> when Carlson wants to shoot his old dog.

Prejudice — it just makes more loneliness...

If you want to look really clever in the exam you could say that prejudice and loneliness are linked because prejudice on the ranch creates loneliness. Don't forget about prejudice against women either — head over to the next page.

Women

There aren't many women in this novel, but they're important. Curley's wife has a big role in the story. The other women help the reader to understand the male characters in the story a bit better.

Curley's wife *is the most important* woman *in the novel*

1) Curley's wife is the only woman who actually appears in *Of Mice and Men*.

2) She's very lonely. She uses her looks to get attention. The men dislike her for it and say she's a "God damn tramp".

3) She has her own dream of being a movie star, but it never comes true. Now she's married to Curley she's just expected to look after the house.

4) In the 1930s, married women were expected to look after their husband's house and have children (see p.7).

> **Key Quote**
>
> Carlson: "Why'n't you tell her to stay the hell home where she belongs?"

Other women *are mentioned in 'Of Mice and Men'*

Although we only meet Curley's wife, Steinbeck describes some other women in the story:

The girl in Weed	**Susy in Soledad**	**Lennie's Aunt Clara**
She's the reason George and Lennie had to run away from Weed. She said Lennie raped her, even though he was just holding on to her dress.	Susy runs a brothel in town. The girls are "clean" and Susy has a sense of humour. This shows what most of the ranch hands are looking for from women.	Aunt Clara looked after Lennie until she died. Then George took over. Lennie seems scared of her — he imagines she's telling him off.

Men and women *don't understand* each other

1) The men in the novel think that Curley's wife is "poison" — they think she's always causing trouble.

2) Curley's wife thinks the men are basically useless. She tells Crooks, Candy and Lennie that they'll never have their dream farm.

3) Curley doesn't understand what his wife needs. His idea of 'being there' for his wife is covering his hand in Vaseline.

4) Curley's wife doesn't understand Curley either. She's not interested in listening to him talk about how much he doesn't like other people.

© Mikki Schaffner

George and Curley's wife.

So, men and women don't understand each other — I'm shocked...

The women who have the biggest impact on the ranchers are prostitutes and a girl who flirts with them to get attention. It's not surprising that the men's opinions of women are a bit mixed up. I like Aunt Clara though — she sounds fun.

Dreams

You'll have worked out by now that no one in the book is very happy. Everyone's missing something. None of them own their own land or home (except the boss). All any of them have are their dreams...

George and Lennie dream of a *better life*

1) George says that <u>most men</u> who work on ranches earn a <u>stake</u> (money) and then go into town and "<u>blow their stake</u>" (waste their money).

2) George and Lennie are <u>different</u>. They don't want to work on ranches <u>every day</u> until they <u>die</u>. George says, "We got a <u>future</u>." They dream of <u>owning their own farm</u> together.

3) This dream keeps them (especially Lennie) going during <u>tough times</u>.

4) We're <u>never</u> really <u>sure</u> whether George <u>believes</u> in the <u>dream</u>:

George tells Lennie about the dream.

© Alastair Muir / Rex Features

Chapter One

George speaks "<u>rhythmically</u>" because he's told Lennie about the dream <u>so many times</u>. He's <u>only</u> doing it for <u>Lennie</u>.

Chapter Three

George is "<u>entranced</u>" (put under a spell) by his own <u>description</u> of the dream. He's starting to think it <u>might come true</u>.

Chapter Five

George tells Candy, "I think I <u>knowed</u> we'd <u>never</u> do her." He realises that the dream is <u>impossible</u> without <u>Lennie</u>.

Some characters have *different dreams*

Key Quote

George says that other farm workers "ain't got nothing to look ahead to".

1) Whit and Carlson are <u>average</u> guys. They make enough <u>money</u> to buy themselves the <u>whisky</u> and <u>sex</u> that they want. They have <u>no dreams</u>.

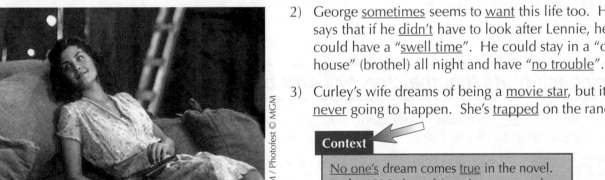

MGM / Photofest © MGM

Curley's wife dreams about being an actress.

2) George <u>sometimes</u> seems to <u>want</u> this life too. He says that if he <u>didn't</u> have to look after Lennie, he could have a "<u>swell time</u>". He could stay in a "cat house" (brothel) all night and have "<u>no trouble</u>".

3) Curley's wife dreams of being a <u>movie star</u>, but it's <u>never</u> going to happen. She's <u>trapped</u> on the ranch.

Context

<u>No one's</u> dream comes <u>true</u> in the novel. In the <u>1930s</u> lots of Americans stopped <u>believing</u> in the <u>American Dream</u> (see p.8).

The trouble with dreams is that they're not real...

Remember that the novel was published during the Great Depression. Most readers of the novel would have agreed with Steinbeck's depressing view of the American Dream (see p.8), which is probably why the book was so popular.

Destiny

Destiny means that something is going to happen and (*Spoiler alert*) there ain't nothing anyone can do to change it. Throughout the book, Steinbeck gives plenty of clues that things are destined to end badly.

The **title** of the book tells us that it's all **destined** to go **wrong**

1) The <u>title</u> of *Of Mice and Men* comes from a poem by <u>Robert Burns</u> called '<u>To a Mouse</u>'. The <u>key lines</u> are:

> The best laid schemes o' mice and men
> Gang aft agley
> And leave us nought but grief and pain
> For promised joy!

This means:

> 'The best plans of mice and men
> Often go wrong
> And leave us with grief and pain
> Instead of joy'

2) This gives you a clue that the <u>characters' plans</u> in the novel will <u>go wrong</u> and this will lead to <u>sadness</u>.

The **characters** have **no control** over their **destiny**

1) George seems to be <u>in control</u> of Lennie's <u>destiny</u> at the end. He makes the <u>decision</u> to kill Lennie, but he had <u>no other choice</u> — "You hadda, George."

2) When Curley's wife was younger she <u>couldn't control</u> her <u>destiny</u>. She was stopped from becoming a <u>movie star</u> because "my ol' lady wouldn' let me". <u>Marriage</u> has <u>trapped</u> her too though — she has to <u>stay</u> on the ranch.

3) Slim has <u>some control</u> over events. He can control <u>small</u> things — like <u>making</u> Curley say he had his hand crushed in a machine. However, he can't stop more <u>important things</u>, like <u>Lennie</u> dying: "I guess we got to get him."

Curley's wife thinks about her future.

© Mikki Schaffner

Steinbeck **hints** that the story will **end badly**

1) Steinbeck <u>leaves clues</u> about what's going to happen later on in the novel. This is called <u>foreshadowing</u>. It suggests that the characters <u>don't</u> have a <u>choice</u> about what's going to <u>happen</u> to them.

Key Quote

George: "I should of knew... I guess maybe way back in my head I did."

2) For example, Lennie's violence <u>gets worse</u> through the novel. He starts by killing <u>mice</u>, then he kills the puppy and he ends up killing <u>Curley's wife</u>. George thinks he should have <u>realised</u> what was going to happen.

Julius Cheeser — he was a mouse with a plan...

Robert Burns did lots of research into the plans of mice. Most of their plans involved stealing cheese by using a series of clever tricks. Burns noticed that the more complicated the plan, the more likely it was to fail. You heard it here first.

Death

Ah... a funny comment about death. I'll just blow off the cobwebs from the 'Big CGP Book of Jokes'... go to 'D'... 'Death'... err... it says, 'There aren't any good jokes about death — it's just too depressing'. Oh well.

Death is a **big** part of the **novel**

1) There's a death in almost <u>every chapter</u>:

Chapter One	Lennie has killed a <u>mouse</u>.
Chapter Two	Slim has drowned four of his <u>puppies</u>.
Chapter Three	Carlson shoots <u>Candy's dog</u>.
Chapter Five	Lennie kills his <u>puppy</u> and <u>Curley's wife</u>.
Chapter Six	George shoots <u>Lennie</u>.

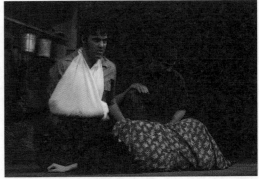

Curley and Slim find Curley's wife.

© Ben Franske

2) This shows that death is <u>part of life</u> on the <u>ranch</u> — nobody can <u>escape</u> it.

3) <u>Lennie</u> is <u>often involved</u> in the deaths in the novel. It suggests that he's <u>dangerous</u>.

The characters **react** to death in **different ways**

When Lennie <u>kills Curley's wife</u>, all the characters <u>react</u> in <u>different ways</u>:

- Lennie sees <u>no difference</u> between killing her and killing the puppy.
- George is <u>more concerned about Lennie</u> than Curley's wife.
- Curley <u>doesn't</u> show any <u>affection</u> for his wife — he just wants <u>revenge</u>.
- Candy is <u>devastated</u> and <u>angry</u> — he's thinking about <u>himself</u>.
- <u>Only Slim</u> pays any <u>attention</u> to Curley's wife and <u>treats her like a person</u>.

Death ends everyone's **dreams**

Key Quote

Candy: "When they can me here I wisht somebody'd shoot me."

1) Lennie's death is the <u>end</u> of George's <u>hopes</u> of buying the dream farm.

2) It also <u>ends Candy's dreams</u> of joining George on the farm. He is now just passing time until he gets the "<u>can</u>" from the farm.

Of Mice and Men is a novel about <u>hoping</u> for a <u>dream</u> even though you're in a <u>difficult situation</u>. When Lennie <u>dies</u>, that hope is gone.

Death — almost worse than a penalty shoot-out...

You can't avoid death... there's a cheery thought. Unfortunately you've got to learn all this stuff because, like death, you can't avoid exams. Revise all these themes, memorise some examples and your exam won't feel like a funeral.

Practice Questions

So, after a section of loneliness, prejudice, crushed dreams and death, I bet you'd like something nice and jolly to cheer you up. Unfortunately, I couldn't get hold of a bouncy castle, but I did come up with these thrilling practice questions to brighten your day. The questions on this page only need short answers.

Quick Questions

Q1   Why are the men on the ranch lonely?

Q2   Who experiences prejudice in the novel? Why?

Q3   Who is the most important woman in the novel?

Q4   Do Whit and Carlson have any dreams?

Q5   Why are George and Lennie different from other farm workers?

Q6   Name two characters who have no control over their destiny.

Q7   How does Curley react to his wife's death?

Practice Questions

Sorry — still no bouncy castle. I did ask CGP headquarters about it, but apparently they're pretty tricky to squeeze into books. Still, here are some more questions to help you through your disappointment. Don't write more than a paragraph for the in-depth questions. Save your longer answers for the exam-style questions.

In-depth Questions

Q1 Why is Curley's wife lonely? How can we tell that she's lonely?

Q2 Explain the role of these women in the novel:
a) Aunt Clara,   b) Susy the brothel owner,   c) The girl in Weed.

Q3 Describe the ways George and Lennie each feel about their dream of owning their own farm.

Q4 What clues are there in Chapters One to Four that Lennie is going to kill Curley's wife?

Exam-style Questions

Q1 a) Look again at the passage in Chapter Three from "'Well, it's ten acres,' said George" to "George sat entranced with his own picture".

How does Steinbeck present the power of dreams in this passage?

Think about:
• The language Steinbeck uses.
• The life they would have on the dream farm.

b) How does the dream contrast with what happens to Lennie and George in the novel?

Q2 a) Explain how Steinbeck presents prejudice in Chapter Four of *Of Mice and Men*.

Think about:
• The character of Crooks.
• The way the other characters treat Crooks.

b) How is this idea of prejudice presented in other parts of the novel?

Language in 'Of Mice and Men'

It's only six chapters long, but Steinbeck has used lots of clever techniques in *Of Mice and Men*.
Writing about the writer's language in your exam will really impress the examiner, so learn these pages well.

Steinbeck's **writing style** is quite **simple**

1) Steinbeck has a <u>simple</u> writing style. For example, when Lennie kills Curley's
   wife, he writes, "she was still, <u>for Lennie had broken her neck</u>". These events are
   more <u>shocking</u> because Steinbeck describes them in such a <u>blunt</u> way.

2) Sometimes Steinbeck uses <u>descriptive language</u> like <u>similes</u> or <u>metaphors</u> to
   describe the <u>characters</u> and <u>setting</u>. For example, he compares the rabbits by the
   pool to "little gray, sculpted stones" to show how <u>still</u> and <u>quiet</u> the clearing is.

Steinbeck gives the reader **hints** to suggest what will **happen**

1) Steinbeck gives the reader <u>clues</u> about what will happen <u>later</u> in the story.

2) This is called <u>foreshadowing</u> — there are lots of examples of this in the novel:

   - The girl in <u>Weed</u> was wearing a <u>red dress</u> just like <u>Curley's wife's</u> red dress.

   - During the novel, Steinbeck shows how Lennie's <u>violence gets worse</u>:

dead mice ⟹ crushed hand ⟹ dead puppy ⟹ Curley's wife dies

3) The novel also has a <u>circular structure</u> — the story <u>begins</u> and <u>ends</u> at the <u>pool</u>. The <u>structure</u> and
   the <u>foreshadowing</u> both suggest that the characters <u>couldn't have avoided</u> what happened to them.

The characters use **realistic language**

George and Slim talk in the bunk house.
© James Cotton

1) Most of the novel is made up of
   <u>conversations</u> between the characters.

2) Steinbeck uses <u>words</u> that ranch
   hands would have used in the
   1930s. This makes the novel
   more <u>realistic</u>.

   "<u>stake</u>" — savings

   "<u>swamper</u>" — cleaner

3) Some of the characters use <u>offensive</u> language.
   Crooks is called a "nigger" and Curley's wife is
   called a "tart" and a "bitch".

4) Steinbeck isn't trying to be <u>offensive</u> — some
   people in the 1930s used language like this.

I thought a stake was something that went well with chips...

Steinbeck makes the ranchers swear a lot, which helps to show that these are people living tough lives in hard times.
Steinbeck doesn't want to make his characters seem more polite and well spoken than they would have been.

Setting in 'Of Mice and Men'

Of Mice and Men is set in a really small area — a few buildings on a ranch, and a nearby pool.
The ranch is typical of the place where men like Lennie and George would have worked in the 1930s.

Most of the story is set on the ***ranch***

1) Chapters Two and Three are set in the <u>bunk house</u>. It's very <u>plain</u>, with "whitewashed" walls and an "unpainted" floor. This shows how <u>basic</u> the men's lives are.

2) The men's things are described as "<u>little articles</u>". They only own <u>small</u> things that they can carry because they're always <u>moving on</u> to find work somewhere else.

3) Crooks has his <u>own room</u>. This shows that he's <u>cut off</u> from the rest of the men. His room has books and magazines which he <u>reads</u> instead of <u>talking</u> to the other workers.

Lennie and Curley's wife on the ranch.

© Ben Franske

The ***pool*** *represents* ***safety***

The novel <u>starts</u> and <u>ends</u> at the pool. Steinbeck describes it <u>differently</u> to show how things have <u>changed</u>.

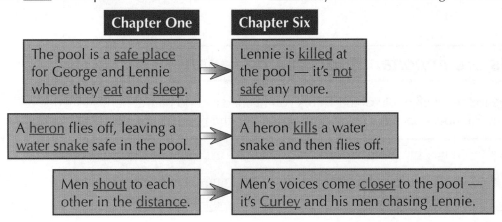

Chapter One	Chapter Six
The pool is a <u>safe place</u> for George and Lennie where they <u>eat</u> and <u>sleep</u>.	Lennie is <u>killed</u> at the pool — it's <u>not safe</u> any more.
A <u>heron</u> flies off, leaving a <u>water snake</u> safe in the pool.	A heron <u>kills</u> a water snake and then flies off.
Men <u>shout</u> to each other in the <u>distance</u>.	Men's voices come <u>closer</u> to the pool — it's <u>Curley</u> and his men chasing Lennie.

The ***place names*** *are meaningful*

These aren't made-up names — they're real places. Steinbeck's keeping his novel as realistic as possible.

1) <u>Soledad</u> is the local town — in Spanish it means '<u>solitude</u>' or '<u>loneliness</u>'. <u>All</u> the characters in the novel are <u>lonely</u>.

2) <u>Weed</u> is where Lennie did a "bad thing" (he wouldn't let go of the girl's dress). A weed is a plant you <u>don't want</u> — it <u>stops</u> nice plants from getting <u>space</u> and <u>food</u>. The memory of the "bad thing" <u>spoils</u> George and Lennie's new life.

My pool represents safety too — it's a paddling pool...

Maybe not the most exciting page in the book, but setting is important in *Of Mice and Men*. Imagine if George and Lennie had just been working in a chip shop on your local high street. It would have been a totally different story.

Symbolism in 'Of Mice and Men'

A good way of getting top marks in an essay on *Of Mice and Men* is to talk about symbolism — the deeper meaning of the book. Steinbeck often uses ordinary things as symbols to get across his message.

Animals represent life in the 1930s

1) In the novel, humans usually <u>get rid of</u> <u>animals</u> when they aren't <u>useful</u> any more:

Symbolism is when an object represents an idea.

- George <u>throws away</u> Lennie's dead mouse.
- Lennie "<u>hurled</u>" the dead puppy away from him in the barn.
- Slim <u>drowns</u> most of the puppies.
- Candy's dog is <u>shot</u> because it's old and smelly.

© Mikki Schaffner

2) The way <u>animals</u> are treated in *Of Mice and Men* <u>symbolises</u> how some <u>people</u> were treated by American society in the 1930s. Back then, if you were too <u>old</u> or <u>weak</u> to be useful your life <u>wasn't valuable</u>.

Carlson takes Candy's dog to be killed because it's old and useless.

Hands are important *tools* on the *ranch*

To <u>survive</u> in the tough world of the 1930s you needed a good pair of hands to <u>work</u>, and maybe to <u>fight</u>. This is why Steinbeck spends a lot of time describing the <u>hands</u> of the characters in *Of Mice and Men*.

Lennie
- Lennie's <u>big, strong hands</u> mean that he's excellent at <u>farm work</u>.
- Lennie uses his hands for "petting" <u>soft things</u>. He doesn't know his own <u>strength</u> and he usually <u>kills</u> the things he strokes.

Curley
- Curley uses his hands to <u>fight</u> but he keeps one soft for his wife — one hand for <u>loving</u>, the other for <u>fighting</u>.
- Lennie <u>crushes</u> his fighting hand, so he can't fight anymore. This makes him even <u>less</u> of a man and even <u>more angry</u>.

Curley's Wife
- Curley's wife's hands are part of what makes her <u>attractive</u>. She keeps touching her <u>nails</u> in front of the men and puts "her hands on her hips" — it shows she's <u>flirting</u>.

Candy
- Candy's <u>missing a hand</u> — if he ever got fired he'd be <u>homeless</u> and <u>useless</u>.

© James Cotton

Curley's wife puts her hands on her hips.

Symbolism in 'Of Mice and Men'

Light and dark symbolise hope and despair

1) As the novel goes on, things seem to get <u>darker</u>. The darkness symbolises <u>despair</u>. Early on there's a <u>warning</u> that "It'll be dark before long".

2) Light represents <u>hope</u>. At the end, the light <u>disappears</u> — "The light climbed on out of the valley". It's the <u>end</u> of the <u>day</u> and the <u>end of Lennie's life</u>.

3) The fading light shows that the <u>hope</u> of the <u>dream farm</u> is fading too.

There are lots of religious symbols in 'Of Mice and Men'

1) Steinbeck uses <u>symbols of religion</u> to talk about important <u>issues</u> and <u>characters</u> in the novel.

2) Religious symbols are related to ideas of <u>good</u> and <u>evil</u>. Steinbeck uses these symbols to describe <u>things</u> and <u>people</u>.

- Slim is described as being a bit like <u>God</u> — he has "calm, <u>Godlike</u> eyes". This makes him seem <u>trustworthy</u> and <u>good</u>.

- Curley's wife wears <u>red</u> which links her to evil and the <u>devil</u>. She <u>tempts</u> the men by flirting with them.

- George and Lennie's <u>dream farm</u> is "Just like heaven". Lennie <u>destroys</u> their dream of the farm when he kills Curley's wife.

Red is used a lot in the book

There are a lot of <u>red</u> things on the ranch.

Red is...

- The colour of <u>danger</u> and blood.

- The <u>only</u> colour used to describe <u>Curley's wife</u>. She has red lips, red nails, and red "feathers" on her "red mules". It suggests that she's <u>sexy</u> but also <u>dangerous</u>.

- The colour of the girl's <u>dress</u> Lennie clung to in Weed. This is an example of the link between the colour <u>red</u> and <u>danger</u>.

© Ben Franske

Curley's wife wears a red dress.

Hand over that rifle — I'm hunting wabbits...

Lennie's hands are both deadly and loving. They stroke and pet first, then they crush, destroy and kill — mice, a puppy, then Curley's wife. He's not aware of what he's capable of — petting and killing get all mixed up.

Practice Questions

The end of another section full of smiles, joy and candyfloss. Oh no, sorry, it's full of doom, tragedy and water snakes. Ah well, better get answering these questions. Then you can have some candyfloss.

Quick Questions

Q1   Why does Steinbeck use words that ranch hands would have used in the 1930s?
a) To make the novel more realistic.
b) To offend people.

Q2   Where does the novel begin and end?

Q3   Write down three different animals in the novel.

Q4   What do Lennie's hands show in the novel?

Q5   Which character is described in a "Godlike" way?

Q6   Name two things in the novel which are red.

Practice Questions

And now, just to mix things up a bit, here are some more questions. I'm just kidding of course — this isn't mixing things up at all. I'm not kidding about the questions though — here they are, exciting as ever...

In-depth Questions

Q1   Why do you think Steinbeck includes lots of conversation between characters in his novel?

Q2   What kind of language does Steinbeck use to describe the bunk house?

Q3   How does Steinbeck use descriptions of light and darkness in *Of Mice and Men*?

Exam-style Questions

Q1 a) How is the setting of the pool important to the novel as a whole?

Think about:
• What the pool represents at the beginning of the novel.
• What the pool represents at the end of the novel.

   b) Which other settings are important in the novel and why?

Q2 a) Read the passage in Chapter Five from "'Look out, now...'" to "'I done another bad thing.'"

How does Steinbeck make this passage tense and exciting?

Think about:
• The language used.
• How Steinbeck describes the action.

   b) Write about one other part of the novel where Steinbeck creates tension.

Section Five — The Writer's Techniques

Assessment Advice

If you're studying *Of Mice and Men* for an exam, this section will help you write a scorching answer. The planning and essay writing advice will be really useful if you're doing a controlled assessment too.

The exam questions will test **four main skills**

The <u>examiner</u> will be looking for you to <u>show</u> that you can:

1) Write about the text in a <u>thoughtful way</u> — <u>picking out examples</u> and <u>quotations</u> that back up your opinions.

> Remember <u>PEE</u> — every time you make a <u>Point</u>, give an <u>Example</u> from the book and then <u>Explain</u> why that example backs up your point.

2) Write about the book's <u>form</u>, <u>structure</u> and <u>language</u>. Show how Steinbeck uses these to present the <u>ideas</u>, <u>themes</u>, <u>characters</u> and <u>settings</u> of the book.

> <u>Sections Three</u>, <u>Four</u> and <u>Five</u> will all <u>help</u> you with this skill.

3) <u>Link</u> the story to its <u>background</u> (i.e. 1930s America).

> <u>Use</u> the information in <u>Section One</u> to work out what Steinbeck was trying to <u>say</u> about <u>society</u>.

4) Write in a <u>clear</u>, <u>well-structured</u> way. From January 2013, 5% of the marks in your English Literature exams will be for <u>spelling</u>, <u>punctuation</u> and <u>grammar</u>. Make sure that your writing is as accurate as possible.

> <u>Plan</u> what you're going to write <u>before</u> you start and always <u>check</u> your work.

Make sure you **know** what to **expect** in your **exam**

You might get some bullet points as part of the question. If you get them, make sure you write about all of them.

The style of question you'll get depends on which <u>exam board</u> you're doing.

AQA	You'll get a <u>two-part question</u>. The first part will be about an <u>extract</u> from the novel, which will be given to you in the exam. The other one will be a more <u>general</u> question. Both parts are worth the <u>same</u> number of marks.
OCR	There will be <u>two questions</u> for you to choose from. One will ask you to comment on an <u>extract</u> from the novel which will be <u>given to you</u> in the exam. The other question will be more <u>general</u>.
WJEC	You'll get an essay question that's <u>split into two parts</u>. You'll have to answer part (a), which will be about a short extract from the novel. You'll then get to choose between parts (b) and (c).
Edexcel	<u>English Literature</u> students get a <u>choice</u> of two general essay questions. <u>English</u> students have to answer a <u>three-part question</u> — one or more parts will be based on an extract which will be given to you in the exam.

The advice squad — the best cops in the NYPD...

Whichever exam board you're doing, the questions will probably ask about the themes, characters and background of the book. Just remember to read the exam paper to make sure you know which questions you'll have to answer.

Structure and Planning

It's easy to panic in the exam — all the more reason to spend five minutes jotting down a cunning plan for what you're going to write before you start. Writing your plan down will help you stick to it and not waffle.

Plan your *answer* before you start

1) If you plan, you're less likely to forget something <u>important</u>.

2) Write your plan at the <u>top of your answer booklet</u> and draw a <u>neat line</u> through it when you've finished.

3) <u>Don't</u> spend <u>too long</u> on your plan. It's only <u>rough work</u>, so you don't need to write in full sentences. Here are a few <u>examples</u> of different ways you can plan your answer:

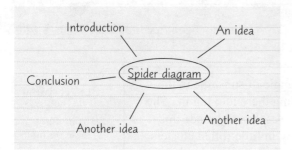

A point in a table...	Quote to back this up...
Another point...	Quote...
A different point...	Quote...

<u>Bullet points and headings...</u>
- Intro...
- An idea...
- The next idea...

Structure your answer

Introduction ⇒ Start your essay with an <u>introduction</u>. It should be a <u>short paragraph</u> which <u>sums up</u> what you're going to <u>write</u> about in the rest of your essay.

Middle section ⇒ The <u>middle section</u> of your essay should explain your answer in detail. Write a new <u>paragraph</u> for each point. <u>Start</u> by making your <u>point</u>, then <u>back it up</u> with an example (or a quotation). Then <u>explain how</u> the example backs up your point.

Conclusion ⇒ Remember to write a <u>conclusion</u> — a paragraph at the end which <u>sums up</u> your <u>main points</u>.

Try to use **examples** and **quotes** in your answer

Always <u>back up</u> your points with <u>examples</u> or <u>quotes</u>.

1) An <u>example</u> is when you describe a bit of the novel to <u>back up</u> what you're saying. ⇒ Curley is an aggressive character. <u>For example</u>, he gets angry with Lennie and George the first time they meet.

2) A <u>quote</u> is where you write down a word or a phrase <u>from the actual book</u>. ⇒ Curley is an aggressive character. When he first meets George and Lennie "<u>his hands closed into fists</u>".

To plan or not to plan, that is the question...

The answer is yes, yes, a thousand times yes. Often students dive right in, worried that planning will take up valuable time. But 5 minutes spent organising a well-structured answer is loads better than pages of waffle. Mmm waffles.

Section Six — Assessment Advice

Extract Question

For some exam boards you'll have to answer a question about an extract from *Of Mice and Men*. The next two pages will show you how to do this, but they'll still be useful if you don't have this type of question.

Here's an **exam question** about an **extract** from the **text**

1) Here's an <u>exam question</u> and <u>extract</u>. It's a good idea to pick out the <u>key words</u> from the <u>question</u> first.

2) It's also useful to <u>highlight</u> the <u>important</u> bits of the extract. <u>Write down</u> any <u>ideas</u> you have on the paper.

> **Q1** Write about how Steinbeck uses <u>details in the passage</u> to show <u>what Curley's wife is like</u>.
>
> You need to talk about the <u>language</u> he uses in the <u>extract</u>. You <u>only</u> need to write about <u>Curley's wife</u>.

Makes her sound young and innocent.

Red = danger. Suggests she'll cause trouble later.

Lots of make-up suggests she wants attention from the men.

Both men glanced up, for the rectangle of sunshine in the doorway was cut off. A girl was standing there looking in. She had full, rouged lips and wide-spaced eyes, heavily made up. Her fingernails were red. Her hair hung in little rolled clusters, like sausages. She wore a cotton house dress and red mules, on the insteps of which were little bouquets of red ostrich feathers. "I'm lookin' for Curley," she said. Her voice had a nasal, brittle quality.

George looked away from her and then back. "He was in here a minute ago, but he went."

She wants the men to look at her.

"Oh!" She put her hands behind her back and leaned against the door frame so that her body was thrown forward. "You're the new fellas that just come, ain't ya?"

"Yeah."

Lennie's eyes moved down over her body, and though she did not seem to be looking at Lennie she bridled a little. She looked at her fingernails. "Sometimes Curley's in here," she explained.

George said brusquely, "Well he ain't now."

"If he ain't, I guess I better look some place else," she said playfully.

Flirting with George.

Lennie watched her, fascinated. George said, "If I see him, I'll pass the word you was looking for him."

She smiled archly and twitched her body. "Nobody can't blame a person for lookin'," she said. There were footsteps behind her, going by. She turned her head. "Hi, Slim," she said.

Slim's voice came through the door. "Hi, Good-lookin'."

"I'm trying to find Curley, Slim."

She's not really looking for Curley, she just wants to talk to the men.

"Well, you ain't tryin' very hard. I seen him goin' in your house."

Suggests she's scared of Curley.

She was suddenly apprehensive. "'Bye, boys," she called into the bunk house, and she hurried away.

George looked around at Lennie. "Jesus, what a tramp," he said. "So that's what Curley picks for a wife."

"She's purty," said Lennie defensively.

Extract Question

When you've read the extract it's time to write your essay plan. And then the actual essay... If this seems like a lot to do in the time you've got, write a practice essay as part of your revision and time yourself.

Use your **notes** to make an **essay plan**

1) Here's an example of an <u>essay plan</u> you could write to answer the <u>question</u> on <u>p.52</u>.

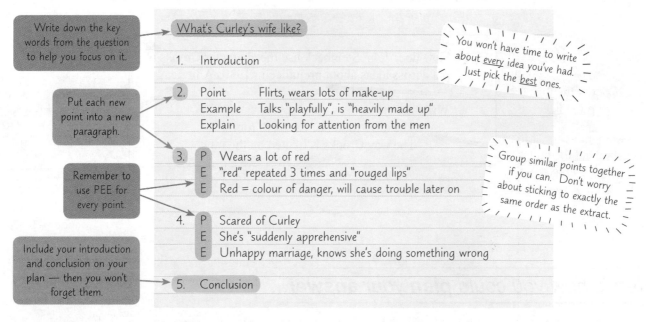

Write down the key words from the question to help you focus on it.

Put each new point into a new paragraph.

Remember to use PEE for every point.

Include your introduction and conclusion on your plan — then you won't forget them.

What's Curley's wife like?

1.   Introduction

2.   Point   Flirts, wears lots of make-up
     Example   Talks "playfully", is "heavily made up"
     Explain   Looking for attention from the men

3.   P   Wears a lot of red
     E   "red" repeated 3 times and "rouged lips"
     E   Red = colour of danger, will cause trouble later on

4.   P   Scared of Curley
     E   She's "suddenly apprehensive"
     E   Unhappy marriage, knows she's doing something wrong

5.   Conclusion

You won't have time to write about <u>every</u> idea you've had. Just pick the <u>best</u> ones.

Group similar points together if you can. Don't worry about sticking to exactly the same order as the extract.

2) When you've <u>finished</u> writing your plan, read the <u>question</u> again.

3) Make sure <u>every point</u> in your plan <u>answers the question</u>.

4) You won't get <u>any marks</u> for points that don't have anything to do with the <u>question</u>.

Use your **plan** to write a **fantastic essay**

Here are some <u>tips</u> for writing a <u>brilliant</u> *Of Mice and Men* essay:

Stick to your <u>plan</u>. Then you won't go <u>off track</u>.

Always write in <u>paragraphs</u>. This makes your essay <u>clearer</u>.

Use <u>short quotes</u> from the <u>extract</u> in your answer.

Be careful with your <u>spelling</u>, <u>grammar</u> and <u>punctuation</u>.

Make sure you <u>explain</u> and <u>comment</u> on ideas and language.

When you've <u>finished</u> writing, <u>check</u> your work. <u>Correct</u> any mistakes.

The best plan for your exam is... to plan

Imagine you're going on holiday. You haven't booked your flights or your hotel, but you think, 'I'm sure it'll all work out when I get there'. What a disaster... Well, that's the kind of mess you'll be in if you don't plan your essay. Trust me.

Sample Exam Question

Now it's time to have a look at an exam question without an extract. The next three pages contain loads of useful tips about how to write and plan a fabulous exam answer, and a very spidery spider diagram.

Here's a *sample exam question*

Read the exam question carefully. Underline the important bits to help you write your plan:

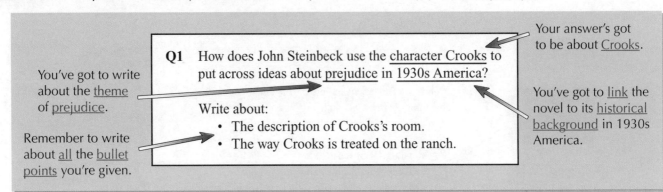

You've got to write about the theme of prejudice.

Remember to write about all the bullet points you're given.

Q1 How does John Steinbeck use the character Crooks to put across ideas about prejudice in 1930s America?

Write about:
- The description of Crooks's room.
- The way Crooks is treated on the ranch.

Your answer's got to be about Crooks.

You've got to link the novel to its historical background in 1930s America.

Here's how you could *plan* your *answer*...

Keep looking back at the question to make sure you're answering it.

If you're given bullet points in the question, remember to write about all of them — you'll lose marks if you don't.

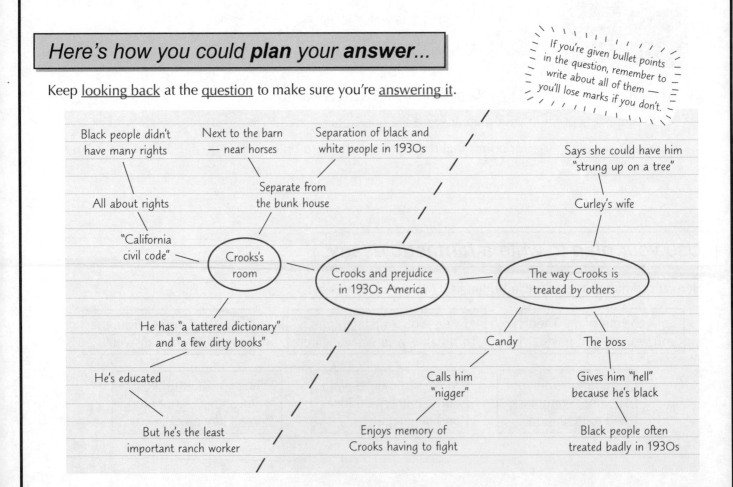

Black people didn't have many rights

Next to the barn — near horses

Separation of black and white people in 1930s

Says she could have him "strung up on a tree"

All about rights

Separate from the bunk house

Curley's wife

"California civil code"

Crooks's room

Crooks and prejudice in 1930s America

The way Crooks is treated by others

He has "a tattered dictionary" and "a few dirty books"

Candy

The boss

He's educated

Calls him "nigger"

Gives him "hell" because he's black

But he's the least important ranch worker

Enjoys memory of Crooks having to fight

Black people often treated badly in 1930s

What do examiners eat? Why, egg-sam-wiches of course...

The most important thing to remember is DON'T PANIC. Take a deep breath, read the question, read it again, write a plan... take another deep breath... and then start writing. Leave about five minutes at the end to check your work too.

Worked Answer

So you've read the question a few times and you've written your plan... Next it's time to actually start writing your answer. Here's some wise advice that'll make it seem as easy as spotting an elephant in a field of sheep.

All answers should start with an *introduction*

1) <u>Start</u> your answer with a <u>short introduction</u>.

> <u>Say</u> what you're going to <u>talk about</u> in the essay.

2) Here's an <u>example</u> of what you could write:

> This essay is about the character Crooks. Crooks is the only black man on the ranch and he is very lonely. He lives on his own in a room attached to the barn. The other characters don't treat him very well because he's black.

3) Everything in this introduction is <u>true</u>, but it doesn't <u>answer the question</u> — it's just a <u>list of facts</u> about Crooks.

4) Here's a <u>better</u> example:

> It's a good idea to use words from the question to link your answer to the question.

> This sentence says <u>how</u> Steinbeck puts his ideas across through Crooks.

> Steinbeck uses the character of Crooks to put across the idea that 1930s America was a very prejudiced society. He thought that this prejudice was unfair. Steinbeck shows this by describing Crooks's room, and showing how different characters treat Crooks.

> This bit says what Steinbeck's ideas about prejudice were.

Start a *new paragraph* for each *new point* you make

1) Every time you make a <u>new point</u>, start a <u>new paragraph</u>.

2) Remember PEE:

Point	Make a <u>point</u> to <u>answer the question</u> you've been given.
Example	Give an <u>example</u> or a <u>quote</u> from the <u>text</u> which backs up your point.
Explain	<u>Explain how</u> the example or quote <u>backs up</u> the <u>point</u> you've made.

3) Here's an <u>example</u> of how to use PEE:

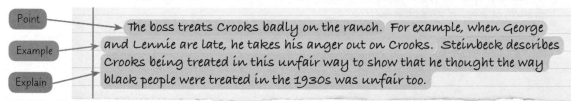

> Point
> Example
> Explain

> The boss treats Crooks badly on the ranch. For example, when George and Lennie are late, he takes his anger out on Crooks. Steinbeck describes Crooks being treated in this unfair way to show that he thought the way black people were treated in the 1930s was unfair too.

Worked Answer

To really impress the examiner you've got to add a few snappy quotes to your answer. Even if you get to take the text into the exam it's a good idea to learn some short quotes so you don't spend too long reading.

Try to use **quotes** in your **answer**

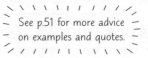

See p.51 for more advice on examples and quotes.

1) Use quotes to back up your point. Quotes don't have to be really long — just a few words is much better.

> Crooks is an educated man. He has lots of books in his room. "And he had books, too; a tattered dictionary and a mauled copy of the California civil code for 1905. There were battered magazines and a few dirty books on a special shelf over his bunk."

This quote is way too long.

2) Instead of copying whole sentences from the book, try to fit short quotes into your own sentence:

These quotes are quicker to copy out (and easier to remember).

> Crooks is an educated man. He has "a tattered dictionary" in his room as well as "a few dirty books". However, the other characters don't listen to him because it's "just a nigger talkin'". They ignore him because he's black.

3) Try to memorise some key quotes so you can easily use them in an exam answer.

4) Start with one for each character and one for each theme.

Character — Slim

"He moved with a majesty only achieved by a master craftsman".

Theme — Loneliness

"Guys like us, that work on ranches, are the loneliest guys in the world".

Leave yourself **time** to write a **conclusion**

1) Keep your eye on the clock and make sure you've got a bit of time left to write your conclusion.

2) Your conclusion should:

- Sum up what you've said in your essay.
- Give a really clear answer to the question.

3) Here's an example of what you could say:

Start a new paragraph for your conclusion.

> In conclusion, John Steinbeck shows Crooks being treated badly by the boss and Curley's wife to show that black people were treated unfairly in the 1930s because of their race. Steinbeck wants the reader to feel sympathy for Crooks and to understand how unfair this kind of prejudice was in 1930s America.

Why do alligators write good essays? Because their quotes are snappy...

It seems like there's a lot to remember on these two pages, but there's not really. Write an introduction and conclusion, start a new paragraph for each new point you make, and remember Point Example Explain. Oh, and pop in some quotes.

Glossary

alliteration | Where words that are close together start with the same sound or letter. | E.g. "slipped twinkling over the yellow sands in the sunlight".

dialect | The way a particular group of people speak, including the words they use. | E.g. The ranchers use language such as, "He's a good skinner. He can rassel grain bags".

foreshadowing | When a writer gives the reader clues about what will happen later on in the story. | E.g. Candy's dog being shot foreshadows Lennie being shot.

imagery | Descriptive language that creates a picture in your mind. | E.g. "the sound of footsteps on crisp sycamore leaves".

metaphor | A way of describing something by saying that it is something else, to create a vivid image. | E.g. "The curls, tiny little sausages".

simile | A way of describing something by saying it's 'like' or 'as' something else. | E.g. Lennie is described as "snorting into the water like a horse".

symbolism | When objects or actions stand for something else. | E.g. The way animals are treated in *Of Mice and Men* represents how workers were treated in 1930s America.

theme | An idea or topic that's important to a piece of writing. | E.g. Loneliness is an important theme in *Of Mice and Men*. The characters represent loneliness in different ways.

Index

The Characters from 'Of Mice and Men'

Phew! You should be an expert on *Of Mice and Men* by now. But if you want a bit of light relief and a quick recap of the novel's plot sit yourself down and read through *Of Mice and Men — The Cartoon...*

George

Lennie

Slim

Candy

Crooks

Curley's wife

The boss

Curley

Carlson

Whit